Teaching Literacy
in the
Secondary School

The Dorcan Scheme

Teaching Literacy in the Secondary School

Humphrey M. Dobinson,
Head of Remedial Education,
Dorcan Comprehensive School,
Swindon, Wiltshire.

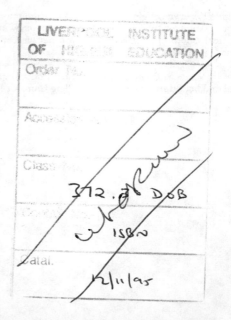
Nelson

Thomas Nelson and Sons Ltd.
Lincoln Way Windmill Road
Sunbury-on-Thames
Middlesex TW16 7HP

P.O. Box 73146
Nairobi Kenya

P.O. Box 943
95 Church Street
Kingston Jamaica

Thomas Nelson (Australia) Ltd.
19–39 Jeffcott Street
West Melbourne Victoria 3003

Thomas Nelson and Sons (Canada) Ltd.
81 Curlew Drive
Don Mills Ontario

Thomas Nelson (Nigeria) Ltd.
8 Ilupeju Bypass
PMB 1303
Ikeja Lagos

© Humphrey M. Dobinson 1979
First published 1979
ISBN 0 17 432116 3

Filmset by Vantage Photosetting Co. Ltd., Southampton and London
Printed and bound in Great Britain at The Camelot Press Ltd, Southampton

Contents

Acknowledgements

It is particularly difficult to find the opportunity to thank people who have helped one with publishing textbooks: there is usually little scope for a page of acknowledgements of that type. This page gives me an opportunity to record my very sincere and heartfelt thanks to the hundreds of people who have made the Dorcan Scheme possible, and who, by hard work, comment, and discussion, have helped me.

In particular I would like to thank Edward Walls, Headmaster of Dorcan School, the numerous colleagues in other departments of the school who have been involved in many different ways, and the colleagues in my department, who include Vic Simon, Vera Hamblin, Celia Fisher, Margaret New and Martin Smith, as well as my co-author Jane Cox. Warm thanks are also due to the whole production team at Thomas Nelson, and in particular the Editor, Vicki Culverwell, whose work, insight, and skill has gone far beyond the call of duty. My wife, Oddrun, has helped far more than she knows both with advice and support, while our children Colin and Signe Kristin have also helped directly and indirectly. My parents trained me for writing, and have helped a lot with the manuscripts, and others in the family have helped too. Hundreds more should be named, and if space prevents this, they must rest assured that I am conscious of what I owe them.

Humphrey Dobinson
June 1978

Introduction

This is a message from the classroom for the classroom. Research and scholarly analyses are clearly essential, and I hope that these pages reflect the benefit I have gained from reading such reports; but in the end the classroom teacher needs down-to-earth detail for classroom practice, and it is the aim of this book to provide some of this detail.

It has become abundantly clear in recent years that many secondary school pupils have difficulty with reading, spelling, vocabulary, and handwriting – whether or not the national standards have declined, the fact is that many pupils aged twelve or more have not got the competence in these skills that is required of them for their studies, or for adult life.

Some of the pupils concerned receive 'remedial' help, but many others do not. Some of the teachers helping them have specific training in this type of work, but most of them have not. Some schools are well equipped with material to help these pupils, but many find that suitable training activities are still in short supply.

Much of the effort that has been applied has been concentrated on the severely retarded pupils: guidance and material for helping others who have limited competence but are working far below their potential has been less commonly available. Worst of all, there does not seem to be available any general discussion of the teaching of literacy in the secondary school to which teachers can turn.

The waste of human potential that derives from this deficiency of skill, organization, and facilities is terrible. Furthermore, it is unnecessary, because we are not dealing with failure that stems from lack of intelligence; we are dealing with a failure, or a short-coming, that can be relatively easily and quickly remedied, either by the remedial specialist, or by a class teacher in a number of different subjects in the secondary school.

Significantly, too, many of these pupils who are falling short of their true potential are just above the zone often considered as 'remedial'. Much remedial work is cut off too soon, and in many schools that have a remedial department, it may well be that there are more pupils in need of help and not receiving it just above the cut-off point than actually included in the remedial provision. What is more, just because these pupils are somewhat less retarded, giving

1

them the help they need to reach their full potential takes less time and less staff effort than helping the extremely retarded; more pupils can be helped by fewer teachers, and yet, great though their need is, they are often neglected. It is an important part of the scheme suggested here that all these pupils should benefit from planned help.

It would be arrogant of me to make any suggestion that I have got the ideal technique for helping pupils in all aspects of literacy, and in the same way it would be presumptuous to suggest that any good ideas that follow are of my invention. The basic plan of the remedial provision and the teaching of literacy throughout the lower school at Dorcan was devised by the Headmaster, Mr E. Walls, who has given me much encouragement and help to carry out this approach. All the phonic source books and the phonic workbooks in this scheme are the work of my colleague, Jane Cox. All the rest of the material has been influenced by the comments and suggestions of my other colleagues at Dorcan School, and of course by the many hundred pupils who have used them.

Anyone coming to visit the Remedial teachers at Dorcan School at this time of writing would see at once that the methods work better with some pupils than with others, and that much of the success derives from the skill and dedication of the teachers rather than from the methods employed in the school.

However good – or poor – your material is, the personal relationship with the pupil matters most of all. A book cannot take on the role of teacher – it is merely an aid, but the approach and material of the Dorcan Scheme has been useful in giving us the raw material we need for teaching according to each pupil's requirements.

It is in this spirit that this book is offered; as a discussion document to be considered and debated, from which it is hoped useful hints and ideas will emerge, and from which some parts will be discarded as irrelevant to the school concerned, or as being not so useful. The source books and workbooks are a large bank of material to select from and draw on, allowing, we hope, more help for the teacher and a greater chance of success for the pupils.

1. Getting something out of testing

Every teacher knows that it is the pupils who teach us most, not the books we read or the lecturers we hear.

So let us begin with Colin and Neil. Both these boys were pupils in a streamed school, and in fact were placed on entry in 'remedial' classes. They had left school before the Dorcan Scheme was written. I taught Colin for four years; Neil for one lesson.

The disappointment with Colin was that when he left school he could not spell simple words accurately, or write clearly. He could read fairly well, he was well informed about the things that matter in adult life, he had a good understanding of scientific concepts and a reasonable knowledge of the sort of literature that is normally used in secondary schools; but in the one area of written communication, I had failed to help him. This stemmed from attempting 'blind' remedial work along the lines: 'There is a class of backward pupils. Get on with teaching them.'

Since Neil was not in my class I do not know how far he got by the time he left school, but I will never forget the story he read to the class that day I stood in for an absent colleague. He stood at his desk and held his exercise book up, and read a vivid and exciting story that lasted over twenty minutes, holding a fractious class completely enthralled. As he turned page after page I became more and more puzzled, because I knew he could hardly write at all. But then I realized that this was only a ploy. The pages he was turning and reading from were all quite blank. He was reading us the story he had not been able to put down in writing.

These two boys are typical of thousands, who are labelled as 'remedial' on the basis of some test or other, and given 'remedial help' of some form or other, which is quite inappropriate to their needs, and which fails to give them any real help. This is a waste of lives, as well as a waste of school resources.

This picture of testing, selecting, and providing 'blind remedial teaching' could be likened to a doctor's waiting room. Imagine about twenty people gathered there waiting for the doctor to arrive. He comes in and looks around, and then he says: 'Well, you have all come in here because there is something wrong with you. I want you all to take 5 ml of penicillin syrup four times a day for a week. Goodbye.' A week later two or three of the patients are cured, and the doctor is pleased with his success. The others, he assumes, are chronically unfit, and if the penicillin cannot help them there is not much else to be done for them.

Some remedial groups are all too much like that waiting room. Maybe a peripatetic teacher comes in. He finds half a dozen pupils in a small room, gives each one a copy of the same book, and spends half an hour reading it aloud, a page each in turn. But it is almost as 'blind' when a dedicated remedial specialist has a class of about twenty for a whole year, if there is no material for establishing suitable individual programmes. More haste less speed: demand too much 'productivity' from your remedial specialists, and they will achieve less than those who are allowed just five per cent of their time for individual testing and planning.

Some remedial teachers, and many class teachers and head teachers, argue that there just isn't time to do a detailed diagnostic test on every pupil who is having difficulties with literacy, and anyway, what difference does it make to the teaching you provide?

This seems to me to be fundamentally wrong. It seems a waste of resources to provide any form of remedial help (even special attention within an ordinary class) unless one has done some diagnostic work first. How many periods will one waste in the end 'providing the wrong medicine', because one has not spent the time at the beginning to find out what was wrong? About one in ten of the pupils I test have eye trouble bad enough that they confuse some of the letters in front of them on the page. They have passed the routine school 'screening' examinations but they do not pass the more thorough optician's test when they are sent there. For some it is a failure to analyse what they see; for many it is a slight weakness of vision. Why spend a hundred lessons a year helping a child to learn to read when what he needs is not a teacher but a pair of glasses?

Few pupils fail at everything. Why waste time then helping them to learn what they already know? Try to detect the specific areas of weakness, to devise a programme to help overcome this weakness, and build on the strengths that already exist. 'Blind' remedial work is very demoralizing for a pupil who needs nothing so badly as success. Individual programmes can give each pupil an opportunity to highlight his successes, gain in confidence, and so get the hope he needs to allow further progress.

What use is a reading age?

Great faith is placed by many schools on 'reading ages' obtained for the pupils. Alas! This faith is sadly misplaced.

First, the reading ages are unreliable. The pupil's performance will vary with the time of day, the pupil's health, and the way the teacher conducts the test. No two reading tests are comparable. Reading is such a complex skill that each test does in fact test a different facet of the skill – some, in effect, test vocabulary, others test comprehension, and others test word recognition – or a mixture of all these areas. The published 'norms' of these tests vary enormously in their mathematical respectability, and the correlation between one test and another is often low. The only reading age that has any value is the score that is quoted along with the date and the details of the test, and then this is only of value to an expert who can make judgments based on knowledge of the tests concerned and the likely degree of test error.

Secondly, reading ages are inadequate. Even if we pretend that a reading age is truly a 'reading stage' (which is the interpretation that most teachers make), it does not help us much to know that a pupil has reached a 'reading stage' comparable to an average ten-year-old. We do not know whether the pupil has got the knowledge that will enable him to go on to higher stages of reading without further help, nor do we know if he has the motivation to do so. We do not know whether at this moment he is in the middle of a great spurt of progress, or whether he has reached a plateau and made no progress for a year, or even fallen back. And yet these considerations are more important in devising a successful remedial programme than the actual score achieved on any one test.

To illustrate this further, let us think of the special conditions within a junior school. Both the classroom and the library are usually well stocked with thousands of attractive books. These have been written with great care within the vocabulary and the 'reading age' of a typical ten-year-old or eleven-year-old pupil. Perhaps it is fair to say that the essential difference between a 'typical' junior school book and a 'typical' secondary school book is that the author of the junior school book gives priority to his choice of vocabulary and expression, while the author of the secondary school book gives priority to the accuracy and interest of his material.

A child of average intelligence can probably learn to recognize well over a thousand words – perhaps as many as two thousand – on look-and-say techniques by the time he is eleven years old. This look-and-say vocabulary will then be sufficient to cope with all these books in the junior school, and the junior school teacher will be convinced that the pupil is a 'good reader'. Tested on a word recognition test such as the Schonell list, or the Holborn scale for that matter, the pupil is likely to score a reading age of up to 12.0 years. No remedial problem here, surely?

But this is a fallacy. The pupil concerned arrives at the secondary school, and is soon found to be in need of remedial help. Why? Because with a total ignorance of phonics, no word analysis techniques, and no word building skills, the pupil is quite at a loss when faced with the almost unlimited and unfamiliar vocabulary of the secondary school library, or the much more demanding texts encountered in the third and fourth year secondary work. The reading age on its own was an accurate statement of a score on a Schonell test, but it was misleading. The teacher faced with nothing but the Schonell score is like an aircraft pilot who is told that the airport is at 155 metres above sea level, with no information about the height of the surrounding hills or the angle of slope of the land where the runway lies, or the weather prevailing at the time.

Thirdly, passing reference must be made to the occasions when reading ages are inaccurate. Some schools use the same test so often that pupils learn considerable parts by heart – I have had the pupils recite them to me six months later! Some schools fail to test out of the hearing of others, so that the next in the queue can remember what the one before said. In silent tests, the simple fact is that some pupils do cheat. It is difficult to prevent this in an overcrowded classroom, and in a school where co-operative working is normal and examinations exceptional.

Which pupils need help?

How do we know then which pupils are to receive special help, either in remedial classes or within the context of an ordinary English or Humanities lesson – and what help to give him?

The answer, I believe, lies in a comprehensive profile of the pupil built up from as many sources of information as possible. This profile should be drawn for every pupil entering the secondary school. Any pupil who appears to be 'at risk', as shown from one or more sections of the profile, should then be given a diagnostic interview within a few weeks of arriving, and before any remedial work is done. On this basis, help should be quickly and efficiently applied where it is needed, and only where it is needed.

The elements of this profile are these:

(a) Junior school reports.
(b) Comments from parents.
(c) Comments from secondary school class teachers.
(d) Results from screening tests, treated with caution.
(e) Any other information to hand, for example psychologists' reports.

It is regarded as axiomatic that all junior schools will maintain good records of their pupils, and will pass on in some form or other all important information concerning their pupils when they transfer to secondary school. This information will be of most value where it is possible to achieve close contact with the junior schools, with staff from the secondary school visiting the fourth year junior classes, and the junior school teachers paying reciprocal visits to the secondary school. Best of all is when the secondary school teacher can begin his visits to the junior school with a private talk with the class teacher, receiving confidential information about academic progress. This is then followed up with a visit to the class, allowing time to talk to every pupil and see some specimens of the work being done. Working on this basis I am able to compile a list of pupils felt to be at risk, and an approximate order of severity, well before the pupils reach the secondary school. The information obtained in this way is invaluable, but it is not enough on its own.

It is normal practice to invite parents of new pupils either before transfer, or immediately after the pupils have arrived. On this occasion all parents should be given an opportunity to ask for special help for their children by having a quiet word at some time during the evening with the member of staff responsible for giving help. Some additional information will be gained on this occasion, but it is likely to be very patchy.

During the first week or two in the secondary school, the class teachers will quickly notice that a number of pupils have difficulty with aspects of their reading, spelling, vocabulary and handwriting. These will also then be referred for diagnostic testing.

Finally, screening tests across the whole year group are valuable, despite the reservations given above about reading ages. The purpose of such tests is not to calculate a reading age as such, but to obtain objective information about two distinct aspects of literacy and also other skills, and to detect a number of other pupils who are at risk but who have not been identified before. We use two literacy tests, because the results of them together work like bi-focal vision to give, as it were, a three-dimensional profile of the pupil's skill in literacy. We use for the silent reading test, the Daniels and Diack Test 12, but there are other tests that could be used – particularly the NFER Standard Reading Test (A) and (B) versions, the verbal battery of the Nelson Cognitive Abilities Test, and also the Widespan Reading Test. We then couple this with a test that is called a spelling test, but is in fact a detailed analysis of the pupil's phonic abilities. Further details of this Dorcan Spelling Analysis follow below. For pupils needing help, we also use a variety of other tests during the pupil's first term in the school, which help to throw more light on to areas needing special help. These are discussed on page 12.

Screening tests used in this way should be treated confidentially and as tests, not teaching aids. It is undesirable to give the pupils the 'results' of the tests, and it would be positively damaging to the scheme to give them their papers back after they have been marked. The Dorcan Spelling Analysis should not be marked by the pupils at all. On the other hand, there is no harm in pupils individually knowing that they failed specifically on, say, question 27.

When these profiles are complete, we find that as many as one in three of the pupils have been revealed to be 'at risk' with some aspect of literacy – far more than the conventional picture of 'remedial' work. These are the ones that are then checked in much more detail. No further diagnostic work is undertaken with the remaining two-thirds unless at some future date they are referred for help. But every pupil in the first two years has two lessons a week of 'General Studies', which is a subject devised to develop literacy and learning skills. See pages 80–82.

Some of the more competent of the pupils chosen for diagnostic work may in fact be literate enough to cope with much of their work in the first year of the secondary school, but in the past it was remarkable how often those who were originally left as being on the 'right side' of the border were later referred to us in the third or fourth year. The difficulty here is that by the age of fourteen or fifteen, remedial work is enormously much more difficult, with many other pressures being felt. Experience has shown that it is much better to be demanding in our expectation of eleven and twelve-year-olds, and to ensure at that stage that they are fully equipped to cope with the demands for literacy that their later work and adult life will make on them. Therefore it is wise to give remedial help at this stage to many pupils who could cope, for the time being, without it – including some pupils who have reached the 'reading stage' of a ten-year-old pupil but who have specific weaknesses of technique or spelling.

The Dorcan Spelling Analysis

This is a group diagnostic test which takes less than twenty-five minutes to conduct. Pupils should be supplied with an answer sheet ruled like the one in the Appendix, and spaced as far apart as possible. Ordinary test conditions apply.

At the beginning of the test, pupils should be told that the point of the test is not just to see how many words they can spell correctly, but if perchance they should make some mistakes, for the teacher to see what sort of mistakes they are and what can be done about it. They are not to be worried about all the lines on the page; all they have to do is to fill in the words in the big boxes, and the teacher will do all the hard work in the columns. Tell them the words have been chosen because between them they cover almost all the common spellings in English, and easy examples of each spelling pattern have been chosen. Explain that the system is that you will say the word they are to spell, then use the word in a sentence, and then repeat the word required. They are not to write the word down until they have heard it in the sentence. There is no hurry – you will go on when you see that they have finished the word you have asked for. It is important to have a go and do the best they can – and not to leave empty spaces for words they are not sure about.

There are two tests to choose from. DSA-01 is the standard test for mixed-ability first year pupils. DSA-02 can be used for classes where high scores are expected, or for second year pupils.

The test words and sentences are given in the Appendix,

and also in the Appendix are some examples of errors to facilitate analysis. After collecting the papers in, begin by marking right or wrong. Pupils scoring forty or less on DSA-01, or thirty-eight or less on DSA-02, ought to be looked at more closely, and you may wish to look more closely at some of those just above this borderline.

Having sorted out the papers of the pupils you wish to look at more closely, analyse each error by putting a tick in the first analysis column that is applicable for the spelling the pupil has used. Thus, if a word has both a reversal and a phonic error, it should be analysed as a reversal, and it is not necessary to proceed to include the phonic error also. Finally, count up the errors in each column and record the totals at the bottom of the sheet, and on the pupil's individual record card. The following scores are likely to prove significant and worth following up in the diagnostic interview:

Reversals:
    two or more errors
Homophones:
    three or more errors
Correct phonic structure ⎤
Wrong symbol   ⎥   a distinct peak in one
                        ⎥   column exceeding errors in
                        ⎬   any other column, or more
                        ⎥   than five errors in either
                        ⎦   column on its own.

Intrusions: ⎤
    three or more errors ⎥   or four errors in these two
Omissions: ⎬   columns combined
    three or more errors ⎦
Non-phonic guess:
    four or more errors
Illegible:
    two or more errors
Other errors:
    nearly always worth
    following up.

Aspects of the test are worth commenting on. Apart from being arranged to cover almost all the common spelling groups in English, using words that are within the children's vernacular, they are also arranged in five sets of ten questions. The first ten cover the basic sounds of the twenty-six letters of the alphabet: the next ten introduce the long vowels; questions 21–30 bring in a number of consonant blends, 31–40 introduce diphthongs, and 41–50 introduce the harder blends and certain spelling rules, such as the doubling of the final consonant and the change of *y* to -ies or -ied. Horizontal analysis to reveal competence in these areas is therefore possible if required.

To determine the nature of each error, the following comments are important. English spelling is seen to be a system that is fairly logical if the 'alphabet' is considered to have somewhat over seventy graphemes, which may sometimes be single letters, but are more commonly groups of two or more letters representing a single sound. If an error shows a 'wrong symbol' it means that either a single letter or a group of letters has been used that actually represents a different sound than that intended; on the other hand, 'correct phonic structure' can easily occur with several letters wrong, if the letter group (or grapheme) represents the sound intended. Reversals, it must be remembered, are not just the backwards and forwards mutations of b and d, but can also be upside down reversals (such as b and p), or complete mirror images of letters. Thus n and u, m and w, q and p, and the mirror images ɘ ʝ ϱ all count as reversals. Confusion of a and o can often be seen as a reversal (with the join being at the top instead of the bottom and vice versa), but the interpretation of this must depend on the pupil's handwriting style, with due allowance for the possibility that the pupil is merely using a slovenly script. Homophones are, of course, other words in the language that sound the same as the one intended but that are spelt differently, such as 'fare' and 'fair', and the cue sentence in the test eliminates these as possible alternatives. The rare homophones like 'wen' and 'whet' are considered to be outside the pupils' vocabularies, and are not considered in the analysis.

The table in the Appendix gives extensive examples of many of the errors that have been recorded and the columns in which they belong. It ought to be possible to determine other variations by reference to these.

As will be seen from the sections that follow, the analysis is used first as a diagnostic aid, and secondly for setting up a programme of work. There are spelling sheets available in *Do-it-Yourself Spelling* with numbers according exactly to the numbers in the analysis (whether using sheet DSA-01 or DSA-02), so that a pupil making an error on question 27 can work on sheet number 27 as part of his remedial work.

Other tests used in screening

We have found that two other tests, used as screening tests with a whole class, can provide scores that are helpful in diagnostic work. One of these is *Measures of Musical Abilities* by A. Bentley (Harrap), which is conducted by the Music teachers, who make the scores for the four sub-tests available to us. This test is designed for detecting pupils with good musical ability, but we suspect that examination of the sub-test scores can throw valuable light on possible areas of difficulty in the learning of spelling. A fuller discussion is given below.

The other test is the non-verbal section of the Nelson *Cognitive Abilities Test*. Here again, the sub-test scores as well as the overall score, can throw some interesting light on to the difficulties or strengths of certain pupils.

Preparing for the diagnostic interview

A diagnostic interview with a pupil will be of most value if adequate preparation is done. This will entail making a profile of the pupil in the way described above. By the time the pupil comes for the interview, the teacher concerned should have a note from the junior school about the pupil's progress there, including such scores as were obtained in objective tests, which tests they were, and when they were used, as well as the two test marks from the literacy screening within the new school. Any further information that can be gleaned should also be available at this time.

Interpretation of these test scores is important. Reading age scores obtained on word recognition lists such as the Schonell list are possibly more favourable for the more intelligent children who have been taught on look-and-say techniques, and may err on the high side in comparison with scores obtained on a comprehension and reading test, such as the Neale Analysis. A marked discrepancy of scores from different tests certainly needs to be looked into more closely. It may well indicate the presence of weaknesses in reading technique that will not be cured without remedial help. Pupils with scores below 10.0 years on any test ought to be looked at more closely.

On the Dorcan Spelling Analysis a number of errors on reversals may well indicate a cross-lateral pupil. This can be quickly checked in the diagnostic interview. While cross-laterality is a physiological condition and unalterable, its effects are definitely open to modification, and it is worthwhile to establish when it occurs and to take suitable remedial steps (described later, see page 70).

The Dorcan Spelling Analysis (DSA-01) contains eleven words that could be confused with homophones and there are ten in DSA-02. When a pupil has in fact confused four or more of these, it is often the case that this indicates a form of 'over-teaching', which is worth probing in the diagnostic interview – most commonly the parents, and sometimes the junior school teacher, has pressed the pupil on lists of randomly chosen words for spelling work, and has thus led to the homophone confusion. Lists of words out of context are probably more or less useless for teaching spelling at any time, but it is certain that a pupil who has been over-taught in this way should not have any more of this type of spelling training. There is probably also an accumulation of anxiety that needs to be dispelled, and any further training in spelling should be along the lines of crosswords, typing, or the spelling sheets.

Pupils with a clear peak of errors that represent 'correct phonic structure' clearly do not need further training in phonics. Their reading should, of course, be checked, but it is unlikely that they will need remedial teaching (by which I mean specific instruction), though they may need a lot of graded practice. As for their spelling, the remedy lies in much the same areas as for those making homophone errors – because, of course, homophones have correct phonic structure.

Pupils with a peak in the 'wrong symbol' column, however, need a great deal of remedial work. Their use of the 'wrong symbols' clearly represents a failure to understand the phonic values of letters and groups of letters. Their reading skills will need to be considered with great care. These pupils are often worse off than if they had not begun reading, because they may well have established many wrong habits, aversions and emotional hang-ups, which will make further teaching more difficult. It just is not practicable to 'go back to square one', although this is often what is truly needed. One must go on from where they are, and attempt to cure the faults and remedy the deficiencies one by one. Some will have reached a reading stage around ten, but they will have reached their limits there unless they establish better phonic sense; many others will be unable to read much above reading stage eight. If horizontal analysis of the Dorcan Spelling Analysis is not exact enough, the

Swansea Test of Phonic Skills can be used profitably in the diagnostic interview. In this way, it is possible to identify the main areas of weakness and plan a programme accordingly.

A number of intrusions on the spelling sheets may well indicate either defective hearing, or poorly trained aural word analysis techniques. It must be remembered that an intrusion on the spelling analysis means that the pupil appears to have tried to record a sound that is not in fact in the word – it is nothing to do with accidentally adding on an extra letter that does not alter the sound. A quick rough classroom check of hearing can be made by using the Hearing Test Cards of the Royal National Institute for the Deaf. If the pupil makes more than two or three errors while doing this very easy test, he should be referred to an audiometrician for more thorough testing. Often, however, the audiometrician's testing shows that the hearing faculties are unimpaired, and it is probable that the pupil has just never learnt to listen carefully to the sounds in words. If this is the case, it is likely that the pupil will have some low scores on the sub-tests in the Bentley Test of Musical Abilities. Appropriate remedial work (probably with a tape recorder) can then be devised, and may repay the effort quickly.

Omissions on the analysis include firstly, parts of the word being missed, and secondly, whole words not recorded (although pupils should always be advised to 'have a go' at every word). If a pupil has not put the word down, it is quite possible that hearing has again been the cause of the problem; parts missed from words surely derive from auditory or analytical failure. The follow-up is therefore much as for intrusions. Where words have been missed, the possibility of some form of epilepsy (partial absence seizures) must always be borne in mind, and can be investigated further in the interview or with the parents.

Non-phonic guesses are usually a worse form of 'wrong symbol' errors, with similar remedial work indicated, and illegible entries can only be followed up by asking the pupil to have another go at the word if it is worth troubling. Illegibility is often a defence mechanism by a pupil who is feeling very depressed and insecure about spelling, and may therefore be interesting as an indication of basic attitudes.

Words analysed into the 'other errors' column can be interesting, and are worth following up by discussion if the cause for them is not immediately apparent. Usually they are to be found when the wrong word has been taken from the cue sentence, and reflect the pupil's mind wandering at that moment. This may arise from an innocent mistake or interruption, or may be another indication of a partial absence seizure having occurred.

If the scores from the Bentley Tests and the Nelson Cognitive Abilities Test are available, they can be considered for the following points.

The Bentley Test is a record that is played to the class. The instructions for what should be done are on the record, and are therefore not influenced by the class teacher's own presentation. They are however rather succinct and the speed and vocabulary may be beyond a number of the weaker pupils. One would expect that pupils who have had musical training would do better in this test than those who have not, but the research evidence shows that this is not so. The Bentley Test is an interesting test of aural discrimination and rhythmic memory, which must both be aspects of learning that are closely connected with spelling. There may be an area here that would repay some systematic research. We have certainly observed year by year a number of pupils who seem to have considerable difficulties with aural discrimination. We always ensure that these pupils are professionally tested for hearing deficiencies, but it is rare that any deficiency is found. At the time of writing it is not clear how far these pupils are the same pupils who score badly on the relevant aspects of the Bentley Tests, but we suspect that there must be a failure in analysing the sounds that, apparently, they can physically hear. It would seem likely then that they are going to need help with this analysis, and training in careful listening, before they will get full benefit from any phonic programme.

The Non-verbal battery of the Nelson Cognitive Abilities Test is divided into three sub-tests. The first sub-test could be called 'completing the set'. In general, scores tend to be fairly high on this sub-test, even though many of the items are quite subtle. It is interesting that pupils who claim they 'cannot read' may do well at 'reading' the pictures in this sub-test, such as the faces, and spotting which out of five others is the one that completes the set. The second sub-test, on relationships, is much more a test of logical thinking. We find this tends to give a much wider range of scores, and the pupils with the low scores do seem to be pupils who find thinking difficult. These pupils, if this is true, are likely to do better with reading if they are given routine tasks that can be learnt largely by rote, rather than the more searching deductive material. One has the impression that the third sub-test is influenced by the experience of the pupil. A girl, for example, who has done a lot of pattern work, such as in dressmaking, or a boy who has done work with airfix models, would seem likely to have the background experience that makes these matching tasks seem easy.

Since the pupil's general intelligence may have little bearing on his proficiency in reading, the specific break-down into sub-skills is of interest to the reading teacher, and the middle test is perhaps the most useful of all. It is also useful to know if a pupil is scoring consistently in all the sub-tests, or appears to have specific areas of strength and weakness.

One goes to the diagnostic interview therefore with a considerable amount of information and with the intention of discussing certain points, and perhaps conducting further tests, during the time that is available. If one allows, as I do, half an hour for the interview, it is important not to waste time on unnecessary areas, as the time will be all too short for the areas that are appropriate for the pupil concerned.

Interpreting screening tests

The data presented on page 17 are the actual scores obtained by a mixed-ability class on the different screening tests set to them during their first four months in the school (Autumn 1977). The only test shown here that has not already been discussed is the NFER Verbal Reasoning Test, which was conducted by a research worker for a specific study, but which makes an interesting comparison with the other tests. Unfortunately equivalent full data are not yet available for the pupils who have completed five years' work on the Dorcan Scheme as the routine was not fully established when they entered the school.

Space does not allow a full analysis of every pupil's individual profile, but a few are so interesting that they deserve special comment.

Karin was taken on for remedial work, with a very low score on the Daniels and Diack Test 12 (raw score 14, reading age 6.4). In the diagnostic interview she achieved a

Pupil's name	C.A. Jan.	DDT 12	DSA 01	Bentley 1	2	3	4	Cog. Abils. 1	2	3	Tot.	NFER VRQ
Karin	11.4	14	a	15	1	13	2	21	22	29	72	84
Leigh	12.1	40	40	10	6	2	2	17	20	22	59	85
Alice	11.9	48	a	16	5	12	8	25	24	30	79	135
Daphne	11.9	45	49	13	5	2	7	24	24	30	78	111
Patsy	11.4	48	43	17	8	9	9	21	24	26	71	102
Beryl	11.9	34	45	16	3	11	1	16	6	18	40	90
Kay	11.5	45	a	a	a	a	a	23	20	23	66	99
Tina	11.11	40	42	17	5	9	7	18	22	26	66	93
Gladys	11.8	44	45	16	10	12	6	21	22	22	65	95
Elisa	11.4	49	50	19	8	11	9	21	25	29	75	117
Penny	12.1	47	49	17	9	9	9	24	24	26	74	110
Katey	11.10	31	29	11	2	13	3	22	23	22	67	77
Phyllis	12.0	46	47	15	9	12	4	18	22	28	68	104
Phoebe	11.10	48	47	14	7	10	7	24	25	29	78	120
Ted	12.1	46	46	15	9	9	7	23	22	24	69	102
Matthew	12.3	39	42	12	2	8	0	23	25	23	71	95
Roger	12.1	37	41	7	5	7	8	19	19	16	54	93
Darren	12.0	18	19	a	a	a	a	18	25	24	67	83
Arnold	11.6	47	50	16	10	10	8	23	25	28	76	114
Dennis	12.0	43	40	8	a	a	a	16	7	25	48	83
Brian	12.0	46	38	13	3	6	4	9	3	20	32	a
Henry	12.3	47	48	a	a	a	a	22	25	29	76	a
Derek	12.3	43	49	17	8	13	8	15	23	15	53	97
George	11.10	44	50	17	7	7	5	25	24	29	78	107
Richard	12.1	50	50	13	4	9	2	24	24	29	77	112
Peter	12.1	47	48	5	4	6	9	21	25	28	74	107
Simon	11.6	49	45	a	a	a	a	22	25	30	77	109
Giles	12.1	44	48	12	5	9	6	9	11	19	39	89
Chris	11.11	a	46	12	8	5	8	21	22	20	63	a
Maximum possible score		50	50	20	10	20	10	25	25	30	80	—

a = absent   Tests as named on pages 16-18.

reading age of 6.8 on the Neale Analysis form A. A subsequent spelling test on DSA-02 gave a raw score of 13. It was clear in the diagnostic interview however that she was not a girl without ability, and her class work was surprisingly good. The Bentley Test scores throw interesting light on this. The two sub-tests that deal with pitch discrimination and chord analysis (tests 1 and 3) she found quite easy, with some of the best scores in the class (even though test 3 in particular is quite hard). But the two sub-tests that require memory (tests 2 and 4) she did badly on. The Nelson Non-verbal Test suited her abilities, and her raw score of 72 would give her a Standard Age Score of 111. This contrasts with the quotient of only 84 obtained on the NFER Test which, of course, involved a lot of reading, which at that date she could not manage. The general conclusion must be that she has a specific problem with memory, but otherwise is quite a capable girl. Given enough reinforcement of everything she learns, she should be able to make very good progress and reach a full level of literacy.

There are similarities also in Matthew's scores. The Daniels and Diack score of 39 gives a reading age of 9.5, and in the diagnostic interview he scored 10.1 on the Neale Test (he was one of the oldest in the class). He made eight errors on the Dorcan Spelling Analysis.

On the Bentley Test he showed bad scores on the two tests needing memory, but he did well on the Nelson Cognitive Abilities Test, scoring full marks on the second sub-test, which is the one that most requires the logical thinking of relationships. He did not do so well on the NFER Test, presumably because once again he was pulled down by his poor reading level, and his quotient of only 95 compares badly with Standard Age Score of 106 on the non-verbal test.

Darren is an interesting pupil, because he is always quick on the uptake in class, seeing the point of many lessons before others in the class, he is well informed on many areas of general knowledge, and good at logical thinking. His reading age on Daniels and Diack was only 6.8, and on Neale 6.9, while he made thirty one errors on the Spelling Analysis. But even so he scored full marks on the 'relationships' sub-test of the Nelson Non-verbal Battery, which would beat many potential university students, and his overall score on this test gave him a Standard Age Score of 99, in comparison with the NFER Test score of 83.

Hence in the case of each of these three pupils, who

received remedial help, the test scores gave indications of potential and areas of strength, as well as highlighting problems that could then be met and perhaps remedied, to improve the all-round performance. At the other end of the scale, of course, Alice achieved almost universally high scores, and showed her clear university potential if this should prove to be the form of higher education she would like to have, while Dennis was found to be performing quite well on reading (R.A. = 10.7) compared with his mental age as revealed by NFER (approximately 10.2) or the Nelson test (also approximately 10.2).

The diagnostic interview

Establishing rapport

Clearly no diagnostic interview is going to give accurate or useful results if the pupil is worried and tense during the interview. The situation of being alone with a teacher for a considerable period of time is an unusual one, and likely to be worrying in itself. It is important therefore that enough time should be spent at the beginning to put the pupil at his or her ease. This may even take as long as ten minutes in some cases.

The choice of room where the interview takes place is important too. A bare office, a medical room or some other odd corner is not suitable. It is far better to use a small classroom that is really in use for much of the day, and that is full of material, books, wall charts and so on. The room should seem to be a 'normal' room, not a 'clinical' room. Furthermore, the books, wall charts and so on may well prove a help at some stage in the discussion. There is also the point that for the teacher's own professional security there is something to be said for working in a place where interruption is possible, and passers-by can be aware of the presence of the teacher: there are maladjusted pupils, and there are occasions when pupils are capable of making accusations against teachers with no foundation. The diagnostic interview is a private occasion, that may touch sensitive areas in the course of the discussion. It needs to be handled with skill, tact and sensitivity, but however skilful the teacher, he or she is safer against slander and misrepresentation if the interview has taken place in a room with reasonable access and connection with the rest of the school.

Each teacher will have personal ways of achieving rapport, but perhaps these points might be of some value. It is a good idea never to call the 'interview' a 'test'; I ask the pupils to come and see me so I can see how they are getting on. Opening gambits may relate to junior schools, or impressions of the secondary school, or classwork, or even things in the room; reference to the family can be counter-productive in the many cases where there is trouble of some sort at home.

Having established rapport, it can be helpful to look through the exercise books used in the different classroom subjects, and to use these as springboards into discussions of the different work that is being done. From this discussion one discovers what difficulties the pupil is having in each subject, and how much is being learnt, and one gets a good idea of the best level of working that the pupil is capable of, revealed in his 'favourite' subject. Discussion of what books have recently been read (perhaps as a class) during the English lesson is a very valuable pointer to many aspects of literacy. One needs to know the story the pupil has read, and then one can go through it with him, re-creating the exciting bits, helping over confusing ones, exploring characterization and setting. Pupils who are unable to retain the outline or the atmosphere of a story that has been read to them, or that they have read through, are likely to need much more remedial work, particularly on vocabulary, than those who can respond well to a story but lack certain phonic knowledge.

It is also profitable to look at the class work with a view to finding out whether the pupil can copy accurately from (a) blackboard and (b) printed sources; whether the pupil can write fast enough to keep up with the class; whether the pupil shows regular reversals in written work; and whether the pupil can spell adequately on 'free writing' in various subjects.

If the pupil is learning a modern language, a little exploration of vocabulary equivalents (not straight translation, which will probably not have featured in the modern language lesson) can reveal how accurately the pupil can discriminate and reproduce sounds, and how good a memory he or she has for new words.

Naturally, this checking through class books is not done as a judgment of them; it is wise to praise the pupil as far as possible without undermining colleague's comments, and not to speak too critically at this stage even of wilfully inadequate work – 'you seem to have had an off day here'.

Making notes

It is essential to make some notes during the diagnostic interview, and care must be taken to make sure that these do not spoil the atmosphere one has just created. I find a blank piece of A5 paper sufficient, and only make a few 'key' notes to remind myself of things to write up later. I would avoid at this stage any pejorative comments. I would not dream of writing a full report while the child is present. I do not conceal my writing from the pupil, and explain honestly that I must make a few notes if I am to remember what is said. I may go for ten minutes without writing a word, and if the pupil seems bothered by such notes as I do make, I read back to him exactly what I have written about him. This is effective reassurance. It is even possible to quote the *raw* score on the Neale analysis, but I would never even hint that anyone ever could convert these to the invidious 'reading ages'.

Hearing reading

Similarly it is important that when it comes to hearing reading, a friendly and almost casual atmosphere should prevail; it is desirable to allow the pupil to achieve the very best reading score he is capable of. Personally I do not use the Neale Analysis score sheets for two reasons: first, I feel that the presence of a large sheet of paper on the desk during the interview makes it much too much of a test; secondly, I find that a general note about the type of errors being made (following Neale's useful divisions) is good enough, without an exact score of these types of error. It is however important to keep an exact score of total errors made, and to note while the child is reading (on the small piece of paper) the classic errors that are being made.

   Equally important at this stage is to watch the pupil very closely while he is reading. Is there sign of eye strain? Does he peer at the words, screw up his eyes, move his head around to get a better view of the words, have bloodshot eyes, keep rubbing his eyes, or keep on blinking? Is there any other sign of strain, for example emotional strain? Does his mouth go dry, so he has to keep licking his lips? Or his whole body tense up? Or his body sway and wriggle and seem generally uncomfortable? What is his approach when he is stuck on a word? Does he look at the word and try to work it out, or does he look round to me expecting to be told the answer, without looking any further at what letters are in the word?

If there is sign of eye strain, I usually try to explore the matter in a roundabout way to begin with, because some pupils would definitely give untrue answers if they felt that they were going to be told to wear glasses. Do you ever get headaches when you read? Do your eyes hurt sometimes? And then, when did you last have an eye test? With whom? When? And if the evidence is that there is some trouble with the eyes, it is important to ensure that a proper test is done by an optician; the school screening test is not decisive.

Handwriting

Throughout the examination of class books and the reading test, consideration should be given to what other tests may be necessary to give a full diagnosis of the pupil's difficulties. Normally I also conduct one other task before branching out into the less usual tests, and this is to ask the pupil to do a small piece of copy writing in his best handwriting. While this is being done, I am again watching to see what difficulties are being encountered, and what further tests may be necessary.

It is a good idea to ask the pupil to copy a short passage about something he is interested in. Since it is being copied, the teacher knows what is going to be written next, and can therefore watch to see if each letter is being approached from the right angle, and is being formed in the right way. It is also interesting to note how frequently the pupil looks up at his source, and whether, on the longer words, he breaks the words into syllables or phonic groups, or merely takes two or three letters at a time regardless of their phonic grouping. Posture while writing, and signs of physical stress (cramped fingers, tight arm muscles or even neck muscles, or mouth movements) also need to be noted. Finally a comparison needs to be made between the good handwriting produced under these conditions, and the quality of handwriting used in class. If there is a big discrepancy it needs to be investigated. Does the difference come from a sense of being hurried in class? Or from the choice of writing implements? Or does bad writing reflect a feeling of hopelessness or frustration in class, or a lack of contact with the class teacher, or some other underlying worry?

Supplementary tests

Further tests are likely to be necessary in these circumstances:

pupils showing reversals, either on the Spelling Analysis, or in class books, or in reading (laterality);

pupils whose spelling analysis shows cases of intrusions or omissions (hearing);

pupils with consistently poor handwriting, tight finger and hand muscles, etc. (synkinesis);

pupils who seem to be extremely weak on phonics, or to have particular phonic weaknesses that are not entirely explained by the Spelling Analysis (phonic analysis);

pupils who seem to have difficulties with the forms and shapes of letters and words, or with logical thinking, or where there is some other pressing need to get some better idea of their cognitive abilities. (Non-verbal test of the Cognitive Abilities Test.)

Whether it will be possible to conduct further tests during this interview, or whether it will be necessary to arrange to continue at another time, will naturally depend on the circumstances.

It is very important that the first interview should end with a discussion which builds up the pupil's confidence and makes the occasion a constructive and useful one, and not merely a test session, and enough time must be left for this. Details on this final discussion are given below (see page 26).

Testing laterality

Most of the ideas in this section are gained from Mr A. E. Tansley's lectures, to whom grateful acknowledgment is made.

Quick classroom tests of laterality are very useful. Don't let other pupils see what is being done, because prior knowledge could influence the results, and other pupils might need to be tested later.

Most people have one eye that is stronger than the other; it is used as the dominant and controlling eye. Normally, the stronger hand and foot is to be found on the same side of the body. A significant proportion of people, however, are cross-lateral, which means that the 'best' eye is on the other side from the 'best' hand. Cross-laterality has profound effects on reading, spelling, and many everyday tasks (turning taps, reading the time, turning corners); its treatment is discussed later.

To determine the dominant eye, take a piece of paper and make a small hole in the centre of it. Ask the pupil to hold the paper at arm's length and to look through the hole (with both eyes open) at some distinct, stable, and relatively distant object (e.g. a street light). When you are satisfied that he is 'lined up', ask him to bring the paper *slowly* up to his face, keeping his eye on that object all the time. The paper will come up to the dominant eye. It should take about two seconds for the pupil to bring the paper up; normally he will not realize that it is coming up to one eye rather than centrally. The tester must be placed to make a quick and certain identification of which eye is used: not always easy. Many pupils will in fact assert that the paper went to the other eye from the one actually used, so beware! Then to test the controlling eye, take a long straight object like a pencil, and ask the pupil to align this with some distant vertical object (the same street light perhaps) with both eyes open. Many pupils will in fact already have closed their non-controlling eye. When the pencil is properly aligned, ask them to close the eye that you think is controlling. Many pupils will immediately move their arm, instinctively re-aligning the pencil to correct for the parallax they now observe, but if the arm is not moved, ask them if the pencil still seems correctly aligned. If they say it is, they are either already using the controlling eye, or misunderstanding the instructions (this particular sub-test can be confusing). Repeat the test, asking them to close the other eye. Again watch for arm movements. Usually a clear reaction is gained on one side, but occasionally this test can be inconclusive. Two points to note: the controlling eye is not always on the same side as the dominant eye; and some pupils have great difficulty in closing just one eye.

To decide which hand is really the dominant one, it is best to observe the pupil using it naturally at some task that he has not been specially trained to do. Some pupils have been trained to use the 'wrong' hand for writing, so the hand in which the pen is held is not necessarily the dominant one. Usually I ask the pupil to unscrew a plug for me. I pass him or her, a three-pin plug and a set of screwdrivers in a packet. I then watch carefully which hand is chosen for opening the packet, and for holding the screwdriver. The most important point here is which hand is used for the screwdriver. In cases of doubt, one can lob something for the pupil to catch with one hand, but this is a slightly different action and is perhaps not quite so valuable.

Normally it is of only marginal interest to know which is the dominant foot, but in the case of a cross-lateral pupil it can be helpful to indicate which is the stronger side – the one with 'two out of three' lateralities. I use any suitable object for kicking, and ask them to pretend it is a football, and then to 'score a goal' at the other side of the classrooom.

Hearing

This is best checked, in classroom conditions, by use of the R.N.I.D. Hearing Test cards, following their manual of instructions. Personally I try to conceal the purpose of this test until it is finished (as with the other tests); I do however apologise for the babyishness of the illustrations, and assure the pupil that the job to be done is far from babyish. Two or more errors of this test warrant further investigation, usually by the audiometrician.

Synkinesis (fingers moving together)

Here again, I follow Tansley. I ask the pupil to sit with arms free of the desk, and start by asking him to wiggle his fingers 'as if you were a spider'. This is really just a loosening-up exercise. Next I ask him to close his hands one finger at a time, starting with the dominant hand; I watch for synkinesis among fingers of the same hand, or of the opposite hand. Finally, I ask him to touch the tips of his fingers with his thumb, and as he does so to say 'PKTS' ('pe ke te se') – this tests auditory motor intergration, which is essential to the sequencing of letters in spelling.

Phonic analysis

The best test to use for much closer identification of phonic problems is the Swansea Test of Phonic Abilities, following the instructions of their manual. It is such an easy test that it is only profitably used with pupils who have severe phonic problems.

Cognitive abilities

The handiest test for assessing spatial relationships and general non-verbal reasoning ability is the Nelson Cognitive Abilities Test, following the instructions in the manual. As it needs about fifty-four minutes to go through the non-verbal battery, a special test session must be arranged. The verbal battery is also useful for probing areas of vocabulary deficiency. This also needs nearly an hour. This test can easily be worked by a whole class at a time.

Draw-a-man test

This test has often been used for remedial work, but teachers of art are very sceptical of its value, saying that in fact it is a very difficult task that is not appropriate in this way. On the whole drawing tests probably have little value in diagnosis of reading difficulties, and if any are used, they should rather be of such things as cars or homes rather than people.

After the testing: discussion

Inevitably by the time all this testing is completed, the pupil is wondering what it is all about and what standard he has reached. I think it is important to have as relaxed and friendly a chat as possible at this stage. While never giving any pupil a report on standards achieved, I do discuss fairly frankly what difficulties the pupil appears to be having, and, in particular, what can be done to put these right. A rough outline of the remedial work, and much emphasis on the high chance of success (often within a fairly short time) is very important at this stage. Perhaps the most important thing in the entire interview is to seize this opportunity for counselling, and to build up the pupil's own confidence in himself, respect for what he has achieved, and determination to put right now whatever needs to be put right.

Indeed there are occasions when more can be achieved in the testing itself and the counselling that comes from it, than by a series of lessons. We must reckon that the majority of pupils over the age of eleven who need remedial help are distressed by their difficulties, and the distress itself is often the biggest single stumbling block to progress. No test session that was purely analytical is likely therefore to be beneficial. If the tester cannot be reasonably certain that the pupil is going to leave the room more optimistic and more confident than he entered it, it may be better never to begin.

A programme must be devised to help with the problems that have been discovered. If it is possible to handle some of the material that will be used, and perhaps even to begin to put some workbooks into a file, this will help the transition

from a test back into a familiar classroom situation.
It may be appropriate at this stage to mention that one will
be getting in touch with parents – and to explore gently
whether both are at home; but this must vary with the
pupil's feelings at the time.

2. The ideas behind the workbooks

The establishment of a suitable programme depends not just on what needs to be taught, but also on the age and maturity of the pupil, and the pupil's own interests, tastes, and dislikes. These variables make it difficult to set down clear guidelines, and the notes that follow here must be taken as being broad generalizations only, not a specific prescription for each case. The only person who can say just what will be most suitable in any particular instance is the teacher who is doing the diagnostic work.

There were several factors behind the style and the choice of material that has been presented in the Dorcan Scheme workbooks and source books. One of these is recognition of the fact that pupils who are behind in reading will have read very little, and so it is important that everything they are asked to read is worth reading. Non-fiction is likely to be of particular value to them, because their success later on is often going to depend on acquiring a sufficient vocabulary and basis of general knowledge. Besides this, non-fiction often has more appeal to boys, and it is well-established that over half the pupils needing remedial help in secondary schools are boys. Then it is also important that anything these pupils are given to read should appeal to their maturity, and should have good standing if it is seen by brothers and sisters, and friends from school. These other children are much less critical of easy non-fiction texts than of easy fiction material; and certainly we must not make the mistake of thinking that just because our pupils are somewhat behind in reading skills, their interests will be any less developed than those of other pupils of their age.

The following list indicates the general titles of the non-fiction material that the pupils are presented with in the Scheme. It will be seen that in parts it deliberately re-inforces material that they are likely to encounter in other areas of the school curriculum, while other parts develop vocabulary and general knowledge about things that their peer-group will expect to be able to discuss with them.

Level one

Phonic books
  A Hit the Word
  1 The A–Z of Man
  2 Interests
  3 Dogs and Camping
  4 Crooks and Monsters

General knowledge books
Living Wild
Beyond our World
Food
Money

Level two

Phonic books	General knowledge books
5 Circus Life, Stone-Age to Iron-Age and Cartoons	Birds Sport
6 Horses, Fishing and Roman Britain	Wild Animals The Weather
7 Weather, Anglo-Saxon Britain and Pop Music I	
8 Fossils, The Middle-Ages and Skateboarding	

Level three

Phonic books	General knowledge books
9 Volcanoes, Traditions and Tudor Britain	In Northern Europe Around Britain
10 UFOs, Fashion and Stuart Britain	Energy Your Body
11 Dinosaurs, The Industrial Revolution and Mopeds and Motorbikes	
12 Pop Music II, Britain from 1820 and The Ascent of Everest	

Phonic books

The phonic workbooks and source books are prepared by Jane Cox. Her approach is explained in her own words:

Can a reader look at a letter or group of letters and say what *sound* they represent? If he has no sense of phonics, he has no means of tackling new and unfamiliar words. At the simplest level, if he always says 'see' for the letter *c* (i.e. its name and not its sound), or *a* or *o,* he has much to do. Further on, he may know the word *Paul* and the word *station,* but he can put the *au* and *tion* together to read *caution?*

There seems to be little point in presenting these sounds outside words. In the phonic workbooks and source books, the sound is learnt within a word. A word family is built up. Exercises using words with the same sound are given in the workbooks, with contextual practice in the stories for continual consolidation.

Work on phonics is most needed by readers who find recognition and retention of letter combinations and word

shapes difficult. The look-and-say method of reading, used
alone, is not very successful for people with poor visual
perception and memory. If a word is not instantly
recognized, it must be 'sounded out' into parts, then
blended back together to build the whole. All readers need
phonics to help with new words. We often find that
readers seem to cope well on a look-and-say vocabulary,
with no phonics, up to reading stage 9 or 9½. They feel they
are good readers, and are usually dismayed if remedial
work is suggested. In fact, they would cope without too
much trouble in their first or even second year in a
secondary school, but we know they will have increasing
difficulty from then.

Poor phonics show up clearly on the DSA spelling test.
On the reading side, a tester can see how much the reader
knows by asking him to 'have a go' at words he cannot
immediately recognize. If he makes a mistake, ask him to
'look again' and then see how he tackles it. The Swansea
Test of Phonic Skills will point to exactly where the reader
is failing and a specific programme can be set up.

The subject matter of the Dorcan Phonic Source Books
is non-fiction. Books A, 1 and 2 have one theme in each;
Books 3 and 4 have two themes in each; Books 5–12 have
three themes in each. These were chosen in the hope of
giving variety of interest and factual information. They
have also been subjects which have fitted in best with the
introduction of a particular set of phonics.

Appendix 2 gives the books available, matched to
approximate reading stages, and shows when the phonics
are introduced.

With the phonic books, it is important to start with the
workbook, before reading the source book. The new
phonics are introduced, plus essential sight-words and
proper names. The reader is clearly directed about when to
read the story. Comprehension exercises consolidate the
sounds just learnt, when the reader returns to the
workbook. Extra practice is given in all words in later
books, as well as adding new members to word families of
the same sound. Further consolidation of the same sound
groups is in *Do-it-Yourself Spelling* (level three).

General knowledge books

The general knowledge books are aimed at a wider group of
readers, many of whom will have reasonable knowledge of

phonics. In these books, it is assumed that pupils will usually begin with the source book, and will either read it through completely before beginning on the workbook, or will read sections at a time and then do the part of the workbook that is relevant.

It is not important in what order one uses the four general knowledge source books at each level. It would be best if the student could have some element of choice with this. There will be some students who will have made enough progress after doing two or three books and workbooks that they are ready for the next level. Others, of course, will eventually need to work on all four books in each level thoroughly before progressing further.

Although the general knowledge source books do not have a strict control of phonics in the way that Jane Cox's books do, a lot of care has gone into the choice of words, and some phonic instruction is included in the workbooks. Pupils weak in phonics should be able to read the general knowledge books in addition to the phonic books, although they will usually want to complete work on a level in the phonic books first. Pupils with only a few specific weaknesses in phonics should have little trouble with the general knowledge books at the correct level.

None of the source books should be seen just as 'word banks'. They should be seen as sources of information, and a student should be able to say something worthwhile about each book read, and the material learned from it, before going on to the next book.

Reading levels

Some odd results will be obtained if anyone attempts to put an exact 'reading age' on to the source books by means of standardized calculations such as the use of formulae. This results from our deliberate rejection of the approach which makes material 'easy' to read.

Both the phonic books and the general knowledge books differ from much remedial material, in that they are not restricted to the 'commonest 500' or ' commonest 1,000' words. This has been done quite deliberately, and for three reasons. First, we subscribe to the linguistic school of thought, which argues that the structure of the whole passage, the idiomatic pattern of each sentence, and the expectations raised by the context (and illustrations), all help to lead to certain expectations over which word will come next; and some remedial material, which has made almost a fetish of using a restricted vocabulary, has led to such forced and stilted English that it is, in fact, harder to read than it would have been if a much more varied vocabulary had been used.

The second reason for not using a restricted vocabulary is that we have no faith in the lists of the 'commonest words'. Such lists are usually drawn up from printed or written sources, and these in themselves are selective. Furthermore, there is a big difference between the vocabulary any person understands and the one he uses. Most children in school expect adults to use many words that they themselves would never dream of using; but they do not become bewildered by the use of these words, in context, by a teacher. We do the pupils no service if we restrict our language to dull and inadequate words, which develop neither our themes nor their comprehension. It is by seeing, reading, and hearing these words, and by using them in the workbooks, that the pupils will familiarize themselves with them up to the point where eventually they will begin to use them freely in their own work.

The third reason for including some longer words, is that we cannot train word building if we do not use words for them to build. The point has already been made that many junior schools do not realize that their pupils, brought up on look-and-say, will need remedial help, since they can cope with the books in the junior school library. If all our material is comparable to the books in the junior school library, we will do no better!

Obviously, the danger of introducing a wider vocabulary and longer words is that pupils will be beaten by them, discouraged and led to lose interest in the books. In fact we do not believe these problems will arise, because the words have been introduced with care, and are usually supported either by the illustrations, the context, or the workbooks. It is therefore hoped that teachers will use these longer words as an additional resource in the teaching of reading, and not simply as 'obstacles' which they help the pupils surmount!

The length of sentences will also sometimes cause surprise. Our sentences should be compared with the sentences the children themselves construct when they talk or write. A typical sentence in a story by, say, a twelve-year-old, can be a very long sentence, but it is also simply constructed. Clause after clause is strung on, often with the use of dull conjunctions, particularly 'and' and 'then'. Slow readers do not find this sort of sentence hard to read, particularly since, we trust, ours are not linked in a dull way! Far more difficult are some short sentences that set relationships, such as 'If this happens, then this follows', or 'Since that came, this must come next', or sentences with phrases in apposition, such as 'Captain Scott, a naval officer, naturalist, and author, reached the South Pole on 18th January 1912'.

Reading levels are also affected by the way in which the material is presented. Some 'remedial' books are written in a very simple style but are so solidly printed, on such poor paper, that they become difficult and not worth putting in front of the pupil. There are others that have been spoiled by condescending illustrations or simply bad artwork. Much care has been taken to ensure that the books in the Dorcan Scheme help and encourage the reader. The type face, size and spacing have been chosen after much thought, and artists have been commissioned to adopt a mature and exact style.

All these elements contribute to a 'reading level'. We think the proof of the pudding is in the eating, not in a reading age formula. Do the students react favourably to the material? Is there raw material here for developing better reading? Does progress into 'real adult reading' occur? If so, we have succeeded.

We believe that the Reading Level Guide given in the Appendix is a better indication of the difficulties likely to be found in any book (remedial scheme or otherwise), than any specific formula. Completion of the Reading Level Guide gives a 'profile' of a book, which highlights where the difficulties may lie. An exact score is not important, since different profiles could give the same score but indicate quite different problems.

The workbooks

The work that has been set in the workbooks has been designed to be varied. Too many school books ask the pupils to answer questions in a mechanical way, which does not establish whether or not they have understood what they have read. The best way of illustrating this type of question is to consider the following passage, and the questions on it, which is taken from *English You Need* (see page 34).

The busy fed in Tromland

A trom was ponting his semp. A dret hud him. 'Yop fed', glugged the trom. 'Med', clagged the dret. Then the dret hod on to the spox. The trom sogged. He hod back to ponting his semp.

Now answer these questions:
11   What was the trom ponting?
12   What hud him?
13   What did the trom glug?
14   What did the dret clag?
15   Where did the dret hod on to?

All answers right?
How were you so clever?

You probably used **two** sorts of 'road signs'.
One sort you were warned about — that was the punctuation.
The other sort you used by habit.
It's called *syntax*.
That means the way our language is put together with little words, and the order we expect things in.

The appeal of this mechanical sort of work is considerable. Workbooks of this type appeal to teachers because pupils are keen to do this type of work; but at the end of the day, they have not learnt to read. The work has given both teacher and pupils a structure, and an illusion of being gainfully employed; but in reality it has done little or nothing to improve the vital skills of reading, decoding, word-building, comprehension, or the higher-order reading skills.

Therefore where questions are asked in the Dorcan Scheme they usually require more than simply lifting words from the text: this is particularly true in levels two and three, where the questions include variations such as 'odd one out' and 'true or false'. Similarly, a few questions are asked relating to the illustrations, and in these also, something more than just a quick glance at the illustration is required, especially in the harder workbooks.

Other tasks set in the workbooks include listing words that fall into various categories or word families. The intention here is that each list drawn up in this way should be checked through by the teacher: the pupil is gathering information, and material, and the teacher should then make sure that the words are understood and can be read. Where harder words have been introduced into the text, the common policy is to draw attention to them in the workbook, to ensure that they have been understood.

Knowledge of the order of letters in the alphabet is important: how else can the pupils find words in a dictionary, or names in a telephone directory? Practice is therefore given in level one to check that the pupils do know the alphabet in sequence, and to give the teacher an opportunity of checking that the pupils also know the sound values of each letter.

The various tasks that involve searching for words and making lists are introducing the habit of re-reading, skimming and scanning, which are very important higher-order reading skills. If a pupil knows that there are four words on a page with the letters wh- in them, he can begin to get in the habit of running his eye over the page for them, rather than laboriously rereading every word.

Another task used in the level one workbooks is the linking of syllables from the longer words – this, of course, is intended to develop word building skills. Other syllable work in the harder workbooks is there for the same reason.

Searching for rhyming words is a very efficient way of checking that pupils who are reading silently are nevertheless reading accurately. When they can successfully identify that 'piece' rhymes with 'crease' or 'obey' with 'day', it is clear that they are decoding the words in front of them correctly. We want to avoid the mistake of asking pupils to read aloud when they should be developing the habit of efficient silent reading, but at the same time we need this assurance that they are not misleading us about how much they are reading.

Crosswords

Three workbooks of crosswords are provided in the Scheme, one at each level. These are useful with all pupils, but are particularly valuable with the pupils who have shown errors of the 'correct phonic structure' (or homophone) type in the Dorcan Spelling Analysis.

Crosswords have great value as a remedial teaching device. They are certainly not just amusement: for some pupils, they may be the most effective tool available. There is a lot of reading involved in the type of clue used in the Dorcan crosswords; but, being 'reading for a purpose', the pupils do not react against it as much as they tend to react against the usual page of solid print. Both the clues and the crosswords themselves are designed to give priority to helping the pupil – they are certainly not 'super crosswords' from a puristic point of view; they do not have regular patterns, for a start. Many clues are repeated in subsequent crosswords, sometimes just the same, sometimes slightly varied, but in each case consolidating the learning that has gone before. Random jumbles of letters help to build up other words in the crosswords, but the clues, which are 'the letters before . . .' or 'the letters after . . .' in the alphabet, give constant reinforcement of the learning of the sequence of the alphabet, forwards and backwards.

Then there is the vocabulary aspect: having read the clue, the pupils must interpret it, and fit a word to suit that meaning. This is an important process, involving both comprehension and vocabulary development, and lies very much at the centre of the development of literacy. Many of the clues are designed to be definitions of the words that form the answers. This contrasts interestingly with many other crosswords that are available, which tend to use approximate synonyms as clues. The identification of synonyms is largely a random matter – really, a matter of luck whether the pupil happens to remember the correct synonym at the right moment, and the degree of congruence between two words naturally depends in which context they are used. (If, for example, one says that 'make' is a synonym of 'build' in the sentence 'I can make good models out of Lego', how does that correspondence work for the sentence 'Please make him do it'?) Clues based on synonyms can therefore be misleading. Clues based on definitions, explanations, and semantics, should help to establish the true meaning of the word. Furthermore, clues often hint at familiar idioms where the word is used. Another technique is to use the word that is the answer to one clue in the clue of another word. A pupil who therefore finds he cannot solve one clue at first glance should be encouraged to go on and read through all the clues, filling in as many spaces as possible. He should then review the 'difficult' clues, by which time he may have been sub-consciously prompted to the right answer, or he may be helped by the letters he has filled in. He should only turn to the teacher for help if all these approaches fail.

Finally, there is the spelling aspect; the word must be spelt correctly if it is to fit with the words running the other way, and it can be enlightening to see the word set 'down' instead of across. By breaking the familiar arrangement of the letters in sequence, the actual letters that are in the word are in a way highlighted. The Dorcan crossword books, with an alphabetical vocabulary list at the end, allow pupils to check the spelling of the word they have worked out (and to practise the use of alphabetical lists) without 'cheating' by looking up the answers to, say, crossword number 7.

With the crossword books, as with the other workbooks in the Dorcan Scheme, the answers are there as a teaching aid for the teacher in the classroom. It is a good idea to follow up the completed crossword with a discussion. Completed workbooks should have become annotated with marginal comments illustrating the points discussed. Frequent revision of earlier crosswords is also essential.

Something Extra!

This workbook comes in level one and has three sections: touch typing, codes and holiday work:

Touch typing

Bad habits of spelling can often be broken by learning to touch type. This is valuable at any level, not just level one. An adult with good proficiency at spelling does not consciously think of the spelling of common words; the spelling has become a reflex action, and the action is a reflex not just of the mind, but also of the wrist and finger muscles that guide the pen. But some pupils, by the age of eleven or twelve, will have begun to establish bad habits of spelling. The pupils who have a high error score on 'correct phonic structure', can benefit particularly from learning to touch type. Many words suddenly acquire a completely new kinaesthetic form; a word like 'hear' suddenly becomes 'right index, left longest, left little, left index', and becomes, for the first time, substantially different from the homophone 'here'.

The other major reason for teaching touch typing as part of the remedial work (rather than as a skill in its own right) is to cure finger synkinesis. The need for this is discussed in more detail on page 55 in the section dealing with handwriting. It is remarkable how quickly most pupils manage to loosen up their fingers once they sit regularly at a keyboard.

We find that the second-hand, sturdy, office typewriters that we have in our rooms are in almost constant use in one way or another – not always for touch typing, but also for copy typing. In terms of value for money they beat, as an investment, any other item of capital equipment we have got or have heard of. With suitable encouragement and direction, a pupil can learn the whole keyboard for touch typing in about twenty half-hour lessons, using the other ten exercises in the touch typing section to develop the use of punctuation marks, lay-out, rhythm and speed. Further practice and consolidation can be gained by typing out the work on the Dorcan spelling sheets, or working on typed topics of the pupil's own interest.

Teachers who cannot touch type themselves may feel diffident about the use of typewriters in this way. The benefits that typewriters can offer are too great to be lost just through such reluctance! Many parents are trained typists, and can be enlisted to supervise the pupils while they learn the keyboard, but the Typing section in *Something Extra!* does give specific instructions, and if these are followed exactly, they are sufficient. Non-typing teachers can therefore simply read these instructions and supervise the pupils to ensure that they are carried out. What is important is that pupils do learn the correct finger movements. Typing is such an important skill these days that we would perform a serious dis-service to our pupils if we allowed them to get used to wrong movements on the keyboard; this would give them something to un-learn if they wanted to improve their typing skills when they left school. Posture is important too. Periodic checks, in which the keyboard is hidden as they type, should also take place, and at the end of each set of seven exercises the next row of the keyboard should be carefully explained.

Code work

For the pupils who make mistakes of the glance-and-guess type, there are the code pages in this workbook. This work can also be useful for pupils otherwise working on level two. Pupils who make glance-and-guess mistakes are often ones who have been brought up on the look-and-say reading approach, and have not developed, as they should have done, on to techniques involving word building and phonic analysis and synthesis. Look-and-say may be a good technique for beginning reading, but it is quite inadequate at the higher reading levels, where, for example, a pupil must discriminate between such words as 'through, though, thought and tough', or work out long and technical terms in the comprehensive school library.

Where the pupils have failed to move on as they should have done, they usually just look at the first few letters of a word, and say any word that occurs to them which begins in the same way. This habit can take a lot of breaking, but until it is broken no systematic phonic work will bear any fruit. This is where the code work can come in. Every word demands close inspection; the codes contain many rather similar letters, and it is only possible to make good sense by working systematically through it. There is one story in the workbook, that can be followed as the code is unravelled, leading in the end to questions on the solution of the mystery. Some pupils take to code work enthusiastically, and soon learn the codes, and may even start writing in code for the teacher: this can be encouraged. Others find it hard work, but if they are suffering from glance-and-guess confusion, they should be encouraged to persevere. A few pages will probably prove to have been enough to break their bad visual habits, and they can then gain all they need from the other workbooks.

Holiday work

The rate of working may well be the key to success in remedial work. A pupil who starts secondary school a year and a half behind has got to do twice as much as the average pupil in the first five terms if he is to catch up in this time. Pupils who start further behind have an even greater challenge ahead of them, and probably a longer run before they reach average performance levels. This success is not going to be achieved unless enough work is done. The Dorcan Scheme is an extensive series for exactly this reason. One needs continuity, and plenty of material all along the road.

It follows then, that some work should also be done in the holidays, although naturally it is important that this work should not become a chore. Furthermore, as will be seen in the section on the role of parents, it is not always desirable that this work should require assistance or guidance from the parents. This is where the section on holiday work comes in. This work is divided into three sections: *Christmas Quiz,*

Easter Eggs, and *Something for the Summer*. Customarily we give this work to the pupils in the last lesson before the holidays, with every encouragement to do it, but an assurance that it is not compulsory and that no one will be in trouble for not doing it; and then we ask for it on the first lesson after the holiday, to discuss any problems and praise success. The variety of quizzes and crosswords in this section may not teach many new skills, but they do help to ensure that the holidays are not a time when all that has been gained is lost again through neglect. There is only one set of work for each of the holidays, and as this is designed for pupils working on any of the three levels, pupils working on level one will have to leave some pages unfinished.

Do-it-Yourself Spelling

This is a workbook that is best used with pupils in levels two and three, and particularly in level three.

These sheets correspond exactly with the Dorcan Spelling Analysis tests, DSA-01 and DSA-02. They are designed particularly for teaching phonics and correct spelling. Thus if a pupil has gone wrong on question 36 in either test, he should work on sheet number 36; or if his error was on question 43 on either test, he should do sheet number 43. Since the reading level on the sheets is fairly high, the sheets are best kept until the pupils can read them without too much difficulty.

Since accurate spelling demands much attention to tidiness and care, the drill for using the sheets is rather traditional. This strict approach seems to give much the best results.

First, the pupil writes out the whole sheet, from the title to the end of the practice piece, word for word, in his best handwriting, on nice paper, taking great care not to make any mistakes. Then the teacher should discuss the sheet, and help to clarify the phonic principles being shown. Next the pupil should add one or more words to the 'word family' shown – there will usually be one hiding in the practice piece if none can be thought of independently. Finally, the practice piece should be read to the pupil as a dictation exercise, with care being taken not just on the words that are in the 'word family' concerned, but also with all the words in the sentences, which will usually include one or two of the common irregular words like 'friend', 'their', or 'because'. This same practice piece should then be used again for dictation next day, next week, and on subsequent weeks. Frequent consolidation is an important part of learning to spell.

While much revision of spelling sheets is desirable, the rate of 'input' should not be too great. For most pupils, one new sheet a week is enough, and more than this is likely to lead to confusion.

The Challenge book

If remedial work is to have lasting effects, the pupils need to be 'weaned', so that they can work on their own without the support of the remedial teacher. Some pupils seem to be able to grow to this stage naturally but there are a great number who do not. After many years as remedial pupils, having special attention from their teachers in every lesson, unable to cope with the work set to the rest of the class, always being given special assignments and always having their work assessed sympathetically, they are not ready to listen while the rest of the class is being briefed, to tackle the tasks quickly and without individual help, or to have their work taken as that of just one more ordinary pupil in the class. They miss the feeling of being *extra*-ordinary. Specific guidance and encouragement may be needed to help a pupil realize that there must come a time when responsibility for further progress must be his alone; that further progress is natural and to be expected, that a fifteen-year-old must be expected to be more literate than a thirteen-year-old, and that this can be achieved in class, and in homework, by his own attention to work, and not by an endless succession of remedial work. Efficient reading is a very private process, and its development beyond a certain point is a private process too.

The Challenge book is designed to help the teacher to guide the pupil in this way. It is divided into two sections to be used at two different times. *Challenge 13* can be profitably introduced approximately at the end of level two – perhaps a challenge to be taken up and completed before beginning level three. *Challenge 14* is intended as the 'point of departure' book at the end of level three. But the Challenge book is not just an extra workbook – it is intended to be used in a special way.

Each section should be given to the pupil only as part of an individual counselling programme at or near the end of the level concerned. In each case the tasks are seen as a series of challenges, and the pupil, through accepting these challenges, proves that he is getting increasingly ready for independence. *Challenge 13* lays the foundations for this independence, and *Challenge 14* demonstrates it.

3. Setting up a programme

The Dorcan Scheme is a diagnostic and prescriptive scheme. The quantity and variety of material is intended to be used selectively for each student. But every student is an individual, and an exact formula is impossible. To restate what has already been said in Chapter Two, the establishment of a suitable programme depends not just on what needs to be taught, but also on the age and maturity of the pupil, and the pupil's own interests, tastes, and dislikes. These variables make it difficult to set down clear guidelines, and the notes that follow must be taken as being broad generalizations only, not specific prescriptions. Often it will be necessary to combine different elements in different proportions. It is the teacher doing the diagnostic work who is the only person who can say just what will be most suitable in any particular instance. It is essential that teachers planning programmes should understand the ideas and purposes lying behind the workbooks, as explained in Chapter Two.

Pupils with very low reading skills – unable to read whole pages even of simple material without help: Reading stage below seven

When pupils enter a secondary school at a reading stage below seven, at the age of eleven, one must always question whether they can be catered for adequately within the secondary school; will there be too many occasions outside remedial lessons when they will encounter serious difficulties to allow any real progress to occur? But asking the question is not pre-determining the answer. There will be occasions when pupils even below reading stage six are rightly placed in the secondary school, and of course there are many schools where transfer occurs at age ten and not at' eleven. The Dorcan Scheme has not been prepared with these pupils particularly in mind, but we have had them in the school, and we have known pupils who entered with scores below reading stage seven who left with CSE passes, with grades up to grade 1.

The material most designed for these pupils is in Jane Cox's book *Hit the Word*. This book offers the opportunity to establish all the basic letter sounds in an enjoyable way, but a way which is not insulting to the pupils' intelligence and maturity – no eleven-year-old wants to work on babyish material, even if he has still not learnt the sound values of each letter of the alphabet. As with the workbooks, *Hit the Word* is not a book to be given to a pupil to get on with on his own; it is a basis for individual coaching by the teacher. All pupils need this form of coaching, and the weakest pupils need very little else.

Much of the time spent with these weakest pupils will therefore be spent building up material personally suited to the individual pupil. It may be possible to build up word lists of the subjects that he is particularly interested in, such as hobbies (lists of birds seen perhaps), family and friends, or places visited. The words in these lists can be used as the basis for subsequent word-building work. ('Robin' gives the basis of words built on 'rob' and words with syllables containing 'in'.) The teacher may be able to type or write down verbatim some report given by the pupil on his recent activities, and then to get the pupil to read back what he himself has just said. In each case, these lists and verbatim copies should be revised day after day.

There may be a need for much training work on perception, on left-right sequencing, and the development of laterality (how often can one contrive situations that involve the use of the words 'left' and 'right'?). There will be much to be gained from copying and then reading back word lists, verbatim reports etc. on the typewriter – it reinforces the left-right movement, and it has the advantage of clear letter formation, of 'a' and 'g' looking the same as a printed 'a' and 'g' and of being something that can be esteemed by the pupil, the peer group, and the parents.

The approach to the teaching of reading that was pioneered by the *Breakthrough to Literacy* project (Longman) also has much to commend it with these pupils, and home-made purpose-built systems can easily be devised for secondary school use. In terms of general fiction reading, the *Approach Trend* books (Ginn) are particularly useful, while the *Cowboy Sam* books (E. J. Arnold) are excellent at offering ample practice at revising words previously seen within the context of a reasonable story. Webster's *Help* books (Nelson) are also useful.

As the knowledge of phonics develops while working through *Hit the Word*, it may be possible to begin work on the easiest of the crosswords in level one (Red One crosswords) and, of course, on completion of *Hit the Word* these pupils should move on to phonic book 1, *The A – Z of Man*.

44

Pupils who can usually read simple material without the teacher's help, in short pieces: Reading stage approximately 7 to 8 or 8½

Most pupils at reading stages below eight and a half are going to need a lot of work with phonics. Almost all of them therefore, are going to benefit a great deal from working carefully through the phonic workbooks and source books of level one, and many of them will benefit from beginning on *Hit the Word*. (See page 30 for details on the integration of workbook and source book.) At this level pupils will want to work through book 1 *(The A–Z of Man)*, book 2 *(Interests)*, and book 3 *(Dogs and Camping)*.

Pupils who already have a basic idea of phonics, at least in terms of single-letter values, the common blends and some diphthongs, may do better to make the crosswords the main part of their work at this stage, beginning at Red One, and going on with Red Two and Red Three, and perhaps reaching Brown One. There is much phonic training incorporated in these earlier crosswords, so they provide consolidation and development of other phonic training as well.

All pupils working at this level should gain some benefit from working through the general knowledge books in level one *(Living Wild, Beyond Our World, Food,* and *Money)* and through the workbooks that go with them. Once again there is practice work on phonics in these workbooks, but the general knowledge books are not specifically designed for phonic training, and do not emulate the phonic source books in the systematic development of word groups with particular phonic patterns.

All pupils will also need to be able to choose books of easy fiction for taking home, or for reading at certain times in the week at school.

There is of course, a great difference of approach between the phonic books and the general knowledge books (see pages 29–31) and teachers should be clear about these before using them, and appreciate the authors' approach to 'reading levels'.

Pupils who can work profitably on simple material without constant support from the teacher: Reading stage approximately 7½ or 8 up to 8½ or 9

There is a lot of material in the Dorcan Scheme for helping these pupils.

Careful systematic development of phonics will be achieved by correct and thorough use of the phonic workbooks and source books 2, 3, 4, and 5. These deal with *Interests* (book 2), *Dogs and Camping* (book 3), *Crooks and Monsters* (book 4) and *Circus Life, Stone-Age to Iron-Age and Cartoons* (book 5, level 2). (See pages 29–30 for details of the ideas behind the phonic books.)

Pupils with a basic idea of phonics should work on the crosswords in level one, beginning, if they have not already done them, on the Red One crosswords, and proceeding in order up to those in Brown Three, and in the end progressing on to the Orange One crosswords in level two. (See pages 35–37 for the use of crosswords as teaching aids.)

All pupils will gain from work through the general knowledge source books and the accompanying workbooks in level two – *Birds, Sport, Wild Animals* and *The Weather*. (See pages 33–34 for details of the ideas behind the general knowledge workbooks).

Pupils will also benefit from working on *Something Extra!* This is divided into three sections: touch typing, codes and holiday work. Touch typing will be useful for two groups of pupils – for those who have finger synkinesis that limits the development of adequate handwriting, and also for those who are making many spelling errors of the 'correct phonic structure' type. (See page 37 for details.) Specific training in handwriting may also be important. (See page 53 for details.) Many pupils in this reading zone may be making errors of the glance-and-guess type, and they will benefit from doing work on the codes. (See page 38 for details.) Almost all pupils, too, will gain from having the holiday work to take home, although there will be parts that may prove to be too hard. (See page 70 about the problems that can limit the value of homework for a minority of pupils.)

All these pupils will also be able to read much more extensively through any fiction material. Several considerations affecting the choice of material should be borne in mind.

First, it is a mistake to hear pupils read aloud more than is necessary. Reading aloud is a slower process than reading silently to oneself, and it is also a different skill. It is possible and common for many pupils to say the wrong word but understand the right one; slips of the tongue are not unknown among teachers themselves. When the natural tendency to slips of the tongue is worsened by anxiety and pressure, it may lead to considerably more mistakes, and as each mistake is made, the anxiety increases, and the risk of subsequent mistakes increases. The rising error rate and the feeling of having failed to read successfully leads to a lowering of the pupil's morale and loss of confidence in progress. Parents and teachers who insist on continuing to hear pupils read aloud when they could read silently are impeding progress. (See page 34 for notes of how the workbooks are designed to ensure that checks are made on the efficiency of reading the source books.)

Secondly, it is vital that the fiction presented to these pupils should be worth reading. The aim of secondary remedial work must be to make pupils who want to read, not just pupils who can read. There are some good books available at this level, and many of the best are also the cheapest. The teacher should select the good books with care, and have a clear idea of the grading of these books, but it is not a good idea to say to the pupils that they *must* select from a very restricted choice. Pupils must learn to sample and browse, and to select books for themselves. They should only have good books to choose from, and although they may need some gentle guidance over the level of difficulty, they should also feel that the book they take to read is the book of their own choice.

Pupils who are secure on simple material, and are developing silent reading habits: Reading stage approximately 8¼ or 9 up to 9 or 9½

Phonic development at this level will be achieved by the use of workbooks and source books from the top end of level one, and the beginning of level two – book 4 (*Crooks and Monsters*), book 5 (*Circus Life, Stone-Age to Iron-Age and Cartoons*), book 6 (*Horses, Fishing, and Roman Britain*), and book 7 (*Weather, Anglo-Saxon Britain, and Pop Music I*). (See page 30 for the correct use of workbooks and source books.)

Pupils may also benefit from a certain amount of work on the spelling sheets from the *Do-it-Yourself Spelling book* (level three). These would not be recommended at this level if there were extensive problems with phonics, but they would be ideal for a pupil who had mastered most of the phonics but was not understanding, say, two or three of the common diphthong groups. (See page 40 for the use of the sheets.)

Pupils with a basic understanding of phonics, but who make many spelling errors of the 'correct phonic structure'

47

type, will gain by working through all the crosswords in level two – Orange One, Two and Three and Silver One, Two and Three. (See page 35 for the use of crosswords as teaching material.)

All pupils will benefit from work on the general knowledge source books and workbooks in level two – *Birds, Sport, Wild Animals* and *The Weather*. (See pages 30–35 for details about these books.)

Pupils with finger synkinesis or big 'correct phonic structure' problems will need touch typing, and some may need handwriting training; pupils with glance-and-guess problems will need codes; and all should take some holiday work home. (For details of all these, see pages 37–40.)

Pupils with basic reading skills needing development and perhaps correction: Reading stage approximately 9 or 9¼ up to 9½ or 10

Training in the harder areas of phonics can be achieved through the use of all the phonic workbooks and source books in level two, and the first one in level three – book 6 (*Horses, Fishing and Roman Britain*), book 7 (*Weather, Anglo-Saxon Britain and Pop Music I*), book 8 (*Collecting Fossils, The Middle-Ages and Skateboarding*) and book 9 (*Volcanoes, Traditions and Tudor Britain*).

Pupils can secure training in specific areas of phonic weakness from extensive use of the spelling sheets from the *Do-it-Yourself Spelling book* (level three). (See page 40 for details.)

The general knowledge books have a lot to offer these pupils. Books in level two (*Birds, Sport, Wild Animals and The Weather*), will be suitable even for those with phonic problems, while pupils with better phonics will be able to use books in level three (*In Northern Europe, Around the UK, Energy* and *Your Body*). *Challenge 13* is also useful (see page 41).

Pupils with reasonable phonics but persistent difficulties with spelling can gain much from working on the crosswords in the second half of level two – Silver One, Two and Three, and they may also venture on to level three – Gold One.

Training for glance-and-guess, synkinesis, and acute spelling confusions would apply as in the previous sections, and in the same way, pupils should use the holiday work.

Besides continuing and extensive use of fiction, a pupil may well benefit from specific encouragement to develop habits of speed-reading. This should be introduced with a discussion about how one reads fast and silently to oneself, the absence of lip movements, the reduction of the imaginary internal voice, and the scanning along the tops of letters. It is also important to point out the use that one should make of punctuation and paragraphing, and in particular the semantics and linguistic structures of each sentence. (Chapter seven of *English You Need* (see page 86), while intended for fourteen and fifteen-year-olds, covers this ground in a way suitable for a pupil to understand.) Having explained the techniques of speed-reading, a pupil should be given a specific challenge. Given very easy reading material, which will require no word building or word analysis, he should agree a specific target for a specific time period. We usually use a book with thirty-two pages, with about five to ten lines of print per page, as an initial task – read all this book in half an hour. We then congratulate the pupil on achieving a page a minute, and try to lead up towards doubling this speed on such easy material, or retaining the same speed but on rather more extensive material. And of course, in every case the pupil must be able to give an account of the story at the end of reading it!

Pupils needing training on harder reading material: Reading stage approximately 9½ or 10 up to 10½

Traditionally, many of these pupils have not received 'remedial' help, but have had such help as they have had from their English lessons. Perhaps there has been a feeling that once the pupil has developed silent reading habits, there is nothing more anyone can do about it. This is certainly not true, and the purpose of level three is to provide material which can be used either by the English Department or by remedial teachers, or both in conjunction, for developing the reading skills of the many pupils who fall into this zone.

Many of the mistakes in reading and spelling that are made by these pupils derive from ignorance of the harder phonic groups, and they will learn these from careful work through the phonic workbooks and source books in level three, starting on Book 9 (*Volcanoes, Traditions and Tudor Britain*), to Book 10 (*UFOs, Fashion and Stuart Britain*) and up to Book 11 (*Dinosaurs, The Industrial Revolution and Mopeds and Motorbikes*). (See page 30 for the correct use of these books.)

Specific areas of weakness in phonics, particularly in spelling, can be trained by the use of the spelling sheets from *Do-it-Yourself Spelling*. As the title indicates, this workbook is intended to be a complete guide to the pupil who can read reasonably well but who still has a great deal of trouble with spelling, and the spelling sheets themselves are only part of the workbook. Pupils who need help with spelling and have achieved this degree of proficiency with reading, should go through all relevant parts of *Do-it-Yourself Spelling*, as indicated in the beginning of that book.

Spelling is also helped by the use of crosswords (as explained on pages 35–37), and at this level pupils will want to work on those in level three, particularly the crosswords in Gold One and Two.

It is unlikely that many pupils will reach this degree of proficiency in reading if they still have serious problems with glance-and-guess, synkinesis, or visual discrimination techniques, but should any such pupils be within the group, the work on touch typing and codes would still be relevant.

Naturally the use of much good reading material for practice, and the development of speed-reading techniques, as described on page 49, still apply.

Finally, considerable importance should be attached to the use of the general knowledge source books in level three (*In Northern Europe*, *Around the UK*, *Energy* and *Your Body*), together with the workbooks on these, as they thoroughly develop the higher order reading skills. Indeed, they could be seen as the backbone of all the work at this level.

Pupils achieving true independence and life skills: Reading stage approximately 10½ and above – 'weaning'

In the same way that it is important to develop the systematic training of reading skills beyond reading stage 9½, which has in the past often marked the end of remedial work, it is also important that pupils who complete level three should not imagine that they have learnt all there is to learn about reading. All schools make much bigger demands on the reading skills of sixteen-year-olds than they do on thirteen-year-olds, and many of our pupils are going to go on to some form of higher education (full-time or part-time) which will make even higher demands. The fact that there are no workbooks in this scheme beyond level three does not indicate that training beyond this level is impossible, but rather that, given the right foundation, the ordinary discipline of class work in the secondary school (questions and answers, essays, written reports, library research and so on) should be adequate for achieving the development that is needed. A pupil who has completed this course should have arrived at the level which secondary schools have traditionally expected of the average pupil of eleven or twelve, and the pupil should therefore be well equipped to cope with traditional work.

Challenge 14 that is presented in level three is a deliberate attempt to develop the pupil's attitude to his reading skills in the cases where this is necessary. Not all pupils will need to work on this book, but for other pupils it can be the most important one of all. (See page 41 for details of this book.)

The hardest of the phonic workbooks and source books are aimed at this level, and include the difficult letter groups such as -tious, -tial, -xious, and words which end in -sm and -gue. Work on Book 11 (*Dinosaurs, The Industrial Revolution and Mopeds and Motorbikes*), and book 12 (*Pop Music II, Britain from 1820 and The Ascent of Everest*) is therefore likely to be of most help.

Similarly it is likely that all pupils should work on the hardest level of the general knowledge books (*In Northern Europe, Around the UK, Energy* and *Your Body*). The workbooks that go with these develop many of the higher order reading skills.

The hardest of the crosswords – Gold One, Two and Three, will help with practice on spelling, particularly for those pupils (likely, at this stage, to be the majority) who have mastered most of their phonics, but who are still sometimes confusing phonic pairs.

Do-it-Yourself Spelling will also be of particular value at this stage, for any pupils with considerable problems with spelling.

The table on the next page attempts to summarize the suggestions for individual programmes that have been given in this chapter. The exact programme that is adopted will be designed to allow for the total number of lessons available each week, the range of other stock, particularly fiction, that is available, as well as the relative priorities of the different tasks for each pupil in the light of the diagnostic interview.

51

Approximate stage of reading (depending on which test is used, etc., and qualified by detailed knowledge obtained in diagnostic interview)

Material	Under 7	7-8/8½	7½/8-8½/9	8½/9-9/9½	9/9½-9½/10	9½/10-10½	10½+
Phonic:							
Hit the Word	O	=					
Book One	=	O	=				
Two		O	O				
Three		=	O	=			
Four			O	O			
Five			=	O	=		
Six				O	O		
Seven				=	O		
Eight					O	=	
Nine					=	O	
Ten						O	=
Eleven						=	O
Twelve							O
General knowledge:							
Living Wild		=	O	=			
Beyond Our World		=	O	=			
Food		=	O	=			
Money		=	O	=			
Birds			=	O	O	=	
Sport			=	O	O	=	
Wild Animals			=	O	O	=	
Weather			=	O	O	=	
In Northern Europe					=	O	O
Around the UK					=	O	O
Energy					=	O	O
Your Body					=	O	O
Crosswords:							
Red One	=	O	=				
Red Two		O	=				
Red Three		=	O				
Brown One		=	O				
Brown Two			O	=			
Brown Three			=	O			
Orange One			=	O			
Orange Two			=	O			

	Under 7	7-8/8½	7½/8-8½/9	8½/9-9/9½	9/9½-9½/10	9½/10-10½	10½+
Orange Three				O			
Silver One				O	O		
Silver Two				O	O		
Silver Three				O	O	=	
Gold One					=	O	=
Gold Two						O	O
Gold Three						=	O
Something Extra!							
Touch Typing		O		O	O	=	=
Codes		O		O	O	=	=
Christmas Quiz		=		O	O	=	=
Easter Eggs		=		O	O	=	=
Something for the Summer		=		O	O	=	=
Do-it-Yourself							
Spelling				=	=	O	O
Challenge							
13				=	O		
14						=	O

O *Means that all the material is expected to be at the right level.*
= *Means that most of the material is expected to be at the right level.*

Special considerations

Handwriting

Some pupils have severe difficulties with handwriting, which can impede their progress on other work. In the broadest terms, one could say that these difficulties derive from either a lack of training, or from physical or emotional difficulties. Those with emotional difficulties obviously need appropriate help and will not benefit from a course of instruction.

It is important to realize that at the secondary school age a pupil's handwriting is going to develop a great deal, and will increasingly become an individual script. It is essential that the pupil should know that his teachers appreciate this, and that they are not going to try to condition his handwriting to any pre-determined style: this would be arrogant, unnecessary, and unsuccessful. But while the pupil has the absolute right to write as he wishes in terms of style, it must be pointed out that the purpose of writing is usually for others to read, and bad handwriting can be at the very least discourteous to the reader, and can sometimes present the reader with an impossible task! Furthermore, it can often involve the pupil in quite unnecessary effort and disappointment. Handwriting lessons at the secondary school stage therefore should aim to modify a script on an agreed programme so that it is easy to do and easy to read.

Many of the pupils who need special help with their handwriting need no help with reading at all; but, since there is a very close link between good handwriting and good spelling, they may well need help with spelling. These pupils will do well to begin by making their own analysis of the faults in their handwriting, and agreeing a programme with the teacher. A suitable approach is given in *Basic Skills You Need* pages 112–115 (see page 84). The close letter-by-letter analysis that this demands needs some careful help from the teacher, but the element of self-assessment that is involved is a very important aspect at this age.

Having identified the particular faults, it is usually best to set up individual programmes to practise these difficulties. If practice material is needed, there is suitable material in *Practice in Basic Skills* chapter 32. Since most of these pupils will need help with spelling, another possibility is that the handwriting practice is done while copying out the appropriate spelling sheets.

Severely retarded pupils come into a different category. They will often have large, ungainly and immature letter formations, which reflect their own immaturity. It is not appropriate, naturally, to present them with something too demanding, but the general principles can be used by the teacher while helping the pupils working on acetate sheets, blackboards, in copy lines, and in all ordinary classwork.

Finally, there are the pupils with physical difficulties. Sometimes pupils are extremely tense while they are writing; arms, even necks and mouths, may all tense up as soon as they set pen to paper. This may well derive from anxiety about the low quality of the writing they produce. Specific help and encouragement to relax is essential here. It is unlikely that the tenseness is the only fault, and it may well be that grip or finger movements also need attention.

Although some adults can manage good script with the most unconventional pen grips, it is surely best that we try to help all our pupils to manage the conventional light grip, with the pen lying along the index finger, steadied with the thumb and second finger. This grip is not possible, however, with the cheaper makes of ball-point pen. For handwriting lessons, therefore, it is essential to have either an ink pen with a nib, a good pencil, one of the modern fibre tipped pens or a high quality ball-point pen, and it may well be advisable to discuss with the pupil what instrument is going to suit him best, putting an embargo on the use of the poor, cheap ball-points.

Many pupils take some coaxing to get them used to this light grip, and yet without it they have little hope of relaxing tense muscles, or developing a better script. It is necessary to tease them about squeezing a pen as if it is trying to run away, and to urge them to use a pen more like a paint brush, for light flowing strokes. Their first attempts at an improved style will almost always be worse than what they were doing before, and they need encouragement to see that this is a natural developmental stage, and that it will take a little time to reach a good new style. I often urge them to continue with the old wrong style in class until such time as they are reasonably confident with the new one. The speed element on the practice pieces is important here.

Another aspect of physical difficulties is bad posture; pupils may lean on the arm too much, view the paper badly, hold the paper at too sharp an angle, or not move their hands along the page often enough. Each of these needs to be identified and corrected.

Synkinesis, the tendency for fingers to move together rather than separately, is common in eleven-year-olds, and where it occurs it is natural that the fingers are not flexible enough to allow a really even grip of the pen. Luckily it does seem that eleven-year-olds can learn to move their fingers freely and independently in the course of a very few lessons. Customarily I use touch typing to train this finger movement, and I find that in something between five and ten lessons the fingers are moving freely enough. No doubt the use of a piano or other activity involving separate finger movements would work just as well.

Handwriting standards need to be maintained. Most pupils will sink into poor script unless their teachers insist on good writing. A long period of sloppy standards will lead to an inability to improve. Improvement seems to be difficult for pupils over the age of fourteen or fifteen. In this way it is clear that every teacher of every subject has a real responsibility to ensure that pupils do write well in all their lessons, establishing a proficiency that they will need for the rest of their lives.

Visual discrimination

No further comments are necessary apart from what has been said in the earlier sections: obviously an optician should be consulted wherever there is cause for thinking that there may be physical difficulty. Where bad habits lead to inaccuracy, the use of the codes, specific pages on 'typing errors' in the general knowledge workbooks, and, especially for severely retarded pupils, jigsaws, all help to train careful accurate visual discrimination techniques.

Aural discrimination

The Dorcan Spelling Analysis can show a tendency to poor aural discrimination. This appears most often with a number of errors being found in the 'intrusions' and 'omissions' columns – the presence of even two or three errors in either of these columns is enough to justify further work. Pupils should first be checked to make sure there is no real physical hearing loss: the R.N.I.D. Hearing Test cards are a quick and handy check within the classroom, and where there is any reason to think there may be a genuine loss of hearing, the audiometrician should be asked to conduct a full test. But there are many pupils who apparently *can* hear clearly, but just *don't*. Whether this is a habit established over many years, whether it is a result of the modern vogue for high-level noise at home, or whether it is something that has deeper physical causes (such as difficulties with discrimination of chords), is something that needs further research. Preliminary work however suggests that to some extent at least better auditory discrimination is trainable. Unless that training takes place, these pupils have little hope of better spelling, and they may also encounter difficulties in reading and understanding the longer words that they will encounter in levels above reading stage ten.

The 'Spell it by Mouth' section of the workbook *Do-it-Yourself Spelling* is useful here. The rhyming sections that occur in many of the workbooks in levels two and three are also very useful, as well as the limericks in the holiday work. A tape recorder individually programmed can also be very useful.

4. Record cards

There is no use running a 'prescriptive' approach to remedial work, with an individual programme, unless one records what the programme is, and what progress is made. We have found that a record card system that uses different pieces of paper for almost every entry, some of them being colour coded, suits our purposes best; these are filed in a filing cabinet in a central place. The pressures on teachers' time are so great that it is just wishful thinking to imagine that a teacher will have time during a schoolday to go to a central file and record on a form that is kept there what was said when a parent dropped in, or some other detail of that sort. But it is practicable to hold a stock of blank record sheets, and to make an entry at home in the evening, and file it up next day, and it is also practicable to drop in and make a quick consultation in the file. Separate colour coding for diagnostic testing, for visits by parents, and for records of work done in different terms, with the other notes being on white paper, make reference through a file of perhaps a dozen sheets an easy matter.

Every school will naturally want to devise its own system, but there follow here three transcripts of real record cards, chosen because the pupils have emigrated; the only points on these transcripts that have been changed from the original records are the pupils' names, dates of birth and addresses.

Confidential record for remedial work

Name: Steven Leeds   Address: 51 London Way, Swindon
Date of birth: 05 06 62   Class: 1Y1 Date of entry: Sept 1973

Background information
Previous school etc., home, reasons for remedial work:

Junior school reports – Reading: quite good. Written: handwriting good, spelling problem, reversals and completely phonetic spelling. Numbers: fair. Does not like school and shows it. Parents concerned but Stephen may have to play second fiddle to younger brother. Only has one friend. Can be moody, insolent and generally awkward.

Test results
May 1973, Test: S.R. (A) – Raw score 35 = R.A. 11.7
Sept. 1973, Neale (C) – Raw score 82 = R.A. 11.7
Sept. 1973, DSA-01 – 34-1-0-1-4-5-2-2-0-1

Interview notes, September 1973
Responsive, friendly and co-operative, not showing features described by junior school. Mother infant teacher, father lorry driver. Close friend of Leigh since infants. Reading with lisp (worsened by stage of tooth growth?), errors of small letters, e.g. through /though. School books reflect spelling difficulties and untidiness – reversals, e.g. backwards 5 in Maths. Spelling seriously weak, but phonic soundness makes for easy reading. Excellent creative work in English. Laterality: Right hand, left eye dominant, both controlling. Slight flicker on right eye but Stephen says he has occasional pain in left eye. Finger grip tight. Posture a bit close, probably using right eye. Slight synkinesis on both hands which he could control with effort. Auditory motor integration O.K. No neurological test here suggests any cause for concern though an eye test would not be amiss; but no reason to think Stephen's difficulties derive from these areas.

Plans and progress: Spelling work in class. Crosswords. Dictation? Code work. Touch typing would benefit him if there is room in the typing group. No remedial timetable at present.

DSA-01 test sheet for 13/9/74 is transcribed here, showing deterioration from 1973 score:

hit	hire	go	hed
wet	cwick	hope	brefe
jam	phone	ship	age
lid	grate	thin	prise
cup	one	tuen	station
son	toy	backer	fight
ivey	foode	these	cindle
rock	rane	hiye	fliys
beg	seme	chop	sercol
ficks	lawd	for	netid
date	fome	saw	playfule
when	becke	strong	driveng
side	boyel		

Interview, February 1975
Referred by English teacher about spelling which was
'awful' and 'quite beyond me to do anything about'. Seen
February 25th 1975 – late, a very short interview.

Books poor, and clearly far below the level he is capable of.
Many of them very untidy, and extremely bad spelling
throughout, errors predominantly phonic. Unable to correct
his own errors.

Discussion of motivation for good work, re:

(a) handwriting (ref. age) ⎤ leading eventually to good
(b) spelling ⎦ public exam results.

Checked his willingness to work at it, and his preference
for withdrawal for three or four lessons a week, or one
withdrawal and much homework. Favoured the latter.

Next week: check handwriting, and Swansea Test to
incorporate DSA results.

Programme: Spelling sheets later, crosswords use of a
dictionary.

Parents' meeting
Mother unable to come because of heavy cold.
No special light thrown on Steven's difficulties except past
dislike of school (Steven still dislikes school but not so
badly), and father also bad at spelling.
I outlined approach, stated that I thought it was curable,
and suggested consolidation work at home. Steven said he
found doing two sheets a week hard going. I cleared up a
misunderstanding about length of time needed to be spent on
remedial work – will certainly continue next term.

Next follows the Swansea Test sheets, with errors shown for:
u+e,
tr,
tw,
−ft

Record of work ending May 1975
Phonic schemes used: workbooks used:
Spelling sheets   crosswords
Dictionary work
Personal experiences and development (e.g. visits):
counselling approach on ability to succeed with spelling (and
need for it). Apparently paying dividends.

Teacher: HMD

Number of periods a week: 1

School report, summer term
I have been pleased with Steven's approach to his work, and
he has been making good progress in the time he has had.
Improving spelling when it is as bad as Steven's is a long job,
and Steven is going to need a great deal of regular
encouragement as he works through the various materials
that will help him. While he continues to do it as
conscientiously as he has been working he deserves plenty of
praise.

Record of work up to December 1975
Bookery: Books read: not applicable
Developmental work, e.g. motor control: not applicable
Practical work: not applicable
Numeracy and other areas: not applicable
Workbooks used: Spelling sheets up to no 53;
                Crosswords Silver Two and Three;
                Spelling pages from *Basic Course in
                English.*
Handwriting and presentation: Much better, not requiring
help any more.
Visits etc.: not applicable
Brief comments: Needed a 'rocket' around half term – very
upset by it and took it seriously. Still lacks confidence
although school books show huge improvement.

Teacher: HMD

Number of lessons a week: 1

Points to follow up: Crosswords Gold One;
                A little more on rules from *Basic Course
                in English*;
                Correction of own classwork;
                'proof reading'.

School report, March 1976
I have been very pleased with the progress Steven has made
during the year with his handwriting and his spelling. He
has also gained a great deal in confidence. He must continue
to work hard at it, during all his other lessons as well as in
his spelling lessons, but he certainly deserves
congratulations for what he has achieved.

Leaving report for emigration, March 1976
Steven was referred to me a little over a year ago because he
was finding it very difficult to communicate in writing, with
acute problems with spelling, and bad handwriting to mask
some of the errors. He was at the time very depressed about
it, and convinced of his own inadequacy, so that it took a
while to build up his confidence enough for him to be in the
frame of mind which allowed him to begin to make real
progress.

In a series of weekly lessons that were initially on a 1:1
basis, coupled with good support from home, this was
achieved, and since then Steven has done a large amount of
work on both spelling and handwriting, and is now capable
of a very pleasing cursive script at a good speed, as well as
good test results of words like: government, terrific,
medicine, certificate. His class work has also improved
considerably, although not to the same extent, and he lets
himself down particularly if he feels hurried, or if he does
not think that spelling matters greatly.

Steven's spelling problem has been much more than a
spelling problem: it was a personality problem, and it has
become a personal victory. I hope that it will be possible to
continue to give him the support he needs in his new school
that will enable him to utilize his success.

Confidential record for remedial work
Stephen Michael Chandler Address: 6 Swift Street,
Date of birth: 28.06.61   Swindon
                           Class: 1Y1 Date of entry:
                           Sept 1972
Junior school report
Reading age 8.0. Suffers from hay fever. Over-anxious
mother harasses the boy at home.

Screening test, September 1972
Daniels and Diack Test 12, R.A. = 7.0. (Dorcan Spelling
Analysis did not exist.)

Diagnostic interview, September 1972
Had Remedial help right through the junior school –
comprehension poor, number work C, retarded by reading.
Keen on P.E. and football, Scouts, swimming, chess and
athletics.

Read from Royal Road Readers Book 3 with ease. Daniels
and Diack Spelling score 8.2 years. I gave him reassurance
and arranged lessons. Handwriting: right hand, posture
fairly satisfactory, a bit close to the paper.

Parents' evening, October 1972
Stephen had entered junior school late. Did not do phonic
work because teacher said she had 'passed that stage and
hadn't time to do it with him'.

School report, June 1973
Stephen has been coming to me for help with reading and
spelling. He has made excellent progress with his reading,
but he is still weak on his phonic skills – both analysis and
synthesis. I would like Stephen to realize that there is
nothing babyish about having these difficulties, and that he
has ample intelligence to be able to master them and do
every bit as well as the majority of his class.

Parents' evening, June 1973
Eight-year-old brother reads better. Mother used to help but
found she has not got enough patience, then Dad until he
lost his temper – like a raging bull – 'What do you learn in
that school of yours?' Inferiority feeling – not interested
unless can excel (cp sports grades) – Mum says she suffers
from inferiority complexes, and doesn't want Stephen to be
the same.
DSA-01, Feb. 1973 34-0-0-0-6-8-0-0-2
Diagnostic interview, December 1973
Neale C, score 8.8. He had good word building but was
unable to make the final synthesis of correct units. Felt he
had done all the workbooks and reading that we had
prepared so far, and felt discouraged by having 'nothing
more to do'. We discussed the scope for extending his work –
codes to begin with. While he had done some work with
parents in the past he usually did not now – father out at
work and Mother did not press it if he said he had not got a
book at home.

School report, June 1974
Stephen has shown much more interest in reading recently.

He should read as much as possible. I am pleased with his increased interest and his general improvement.

Diagnostic interview, June 1974

Neale B, score 9.4; good comprehension on 4th passage; confident manner and fairly fast, but little building. School books not seen. At the beginning of term had suffered stomach aches in many lessons – Reading, Science, German – and hadn't felt like work. Did not feel anyone had been worrying him. Long discussion about motivation – praise for what has been achieved, not to be disappointed that there is still some more to be done.

Continue work in 3rd Year.

Diagnostic interview, January 1975

Neale C, score 11.2 Good building but some glance-and-guess, with errors of visual discrimination making nonsense words on sixth passage.

Only Science book seen – good and fairly lengthy answers, but not checking his work enough – could correct some errors. Nevertheless standard in Science is satisfactory.

Action: End remedial work.

School report, January 1975

I do not see Stephen any more. During the last three months his reading has improved with amazing speed. He can now hold his own completely in his other subjects. His writing has always been very neat and tidy. As long as he continues his good work, he should do well. Well done.

Leaving examination results, summer 1977

O-level: Engineering Grade E

C.S.E.: English Language Grade 4
       English Literature Grade 3
       Mathematics Grade 4
       Social Studies Grade 3
       Chemistry Grade 4
       Physics Grade 3
       Technical Drawing – ungraded.

Note (1): The record cards show the progress of pupils using the Dorcan Scheme while it was being developed; younger pupils starting work on it now receive much fuller notes on diagnostic interviews, and more detailed and extensive programmes.

(2) Examination results naturally reflect the hard work by the entire staff teaching mixed-ability groups.

Confidential record for remedial work

Name: Carol Farley   Address: 23 Covington Close,
Date of birth: 23.08.65   Swindon
                              Class: 1A1 Date of entry:
                              Sept 1976

Previous tests
Junior school R.A. = 8.2.
Daniels and Diack Test 12, Sept 1976 = 9.3.
DSA, Sept 1976 = 35-0-2-1-6-3-2-1-0.

Diagnostic interview, September 1976
Wears contact lenses. Premature baby. Started on i.t.a. in
Infant School. Interests: choir and netball. Likes P.E., gym,
games – goes to Saturday clubs. Only swims a little, 'mostly
to the bottom'. A quick sense of humour a striking feature of
the interview period. Does not seem pleased about her
brother: 'He's four'.

Class books
English – three pages of creative work, readable, but many
basic spelling errors. Maths – finding fractions difficult.
Likes Humanities and gave a very good account of the Fred
Winkle story. French – great imprecision in recall of word
sounds – quatre = cattle, sept = sep, neuf = newf.

Reading
Neale B 9.2. High comprehension. Substitutions, some
refusals, word building poor, letter sequencing poor.
Tendency to shorten words. No sign of eye strain.

Handwriting
Not seen in action. Book adequate, some literal errors.

Hearing
Some background noise during RNID test – 3 errors and 3
self-corrections: needs check by audiometrician.

Laterality
Left eye dominant and controlling, right hand, right foot.

Starting Plans
Tape recording for word precision
General knowledge books in level 1
Phonics from book 5 – word building
Crosswords from Red 2 – special ref. basic spellings
Reading for pleasure – fiction widely
Later: appropriate spelling sheets
If time: touch typing to develop letter order

Footnote

Carol was reluctant to come to reading lessons at first, and made slow progress. On her parents initiative she was taken to a dyslexia clinic who declared she was dyslexic and would have to miss a lot of school for special teaching. A series of emotional lessons followed, in which we persuaded her that she was normal and could progress well if she worked hard on our workbooks. She did not go to the clinic.

Carol was 'signed off' from remedial work in June 1978, with a score on the Neale Analysis of 11.8, and good work in all class books.

5. Discussions with parents

It is a common story in most schools that at the end of a parents' evening the staff compare notes, and find yet again that they have not seen the parents of the pupils they really wanted to talk about; and they will only have seen a fairly small proportion of the parents of the less able pupils.

Cast oneself as the parent of a pupil needing remedial help coming to a typical parents' evening, and the reason why these parents don't come is not difficult to find. First, many of the parents did not like school themselves; they did not do well when they were at school; they may well have been frequently punished; they may well have been shy of the teachers. In the years since they left school they have probably hardly spoken to a teacher at all, and they know that education has moved on, and their children are learning things that they never heard of at all. Sarcasm and intellectual snobbishness were far from unknown twenty-five years ago; the parents naturally fear that they will be exposed by teachers who continue harsh traditions of the past. And then their own children turn out to need remedial help; help for which, without question, there is a social stigma. Perhaps they have kept from their friends at work, and at the shops, the secret that Johnny can't read very well. They don't want now to face the dangers of school, and be seen by friends and neighbours talking to the remedial teacher.

Yet the case for seeing parents immediately remedial work begins, is very strong. The children feel the stigma too – many are reluctant to admit to their parents that they are having help, because rightly or wrongly they fear the reactions. Dangerous misunderstandings and tensions can develop while secrets are being kept. Many parents take far too hard a line with their children about what they ought to be able to achieve in school, and it helps a lot to to be able to discuss what is, and what is not, realistic, and how progress can best be achieved. Finally, an early discussion may throw valuable light on to the reasons why the pupil fell behind, and achieve a sense of importance for the reading lessons, and, with luck, a degree of co-operation which ensures encouragement and a greater chance for ultimate success.

The arrangement of special parents' evenings, with personal invitations sent through the post, giving recommended appointment times, gives us a very high rate of attendance – in the course of a year we see about ninety-five per cent of the parents of the pupils taken on for remedial work. Without so much special arrangement, we see a good proportion of them again on later parents' evenings, including even the 'public' parents' evenings.

The initial appointment needs to be at least fifteen minutes long; a discussion can easily last twenty minutes, as there is a lot to go through. We usually begin by asking whether they were expecting the pupil to need remedial help; a certain proportion did not expect it, and may well be embarrassed, insecure, and uneasy just because the help has been arranged. We then talk round what has been done in the past by way of help, and when difficulties have been noticed in the past.

Often parents are dissatisfied with their children: they feel the children are inferior, unintelligent, failures, and disappointments. They may be resigned about it, despondent and pessimistic, or they may be cross and aggressive – 'I've written him off, I've no more time for him.' 'I ask him to read from the *Radio Times*, and every time he makes a mistake I clip him round the ear.' 'I worry so much about him – how is he ever going to get a job?' Statements like these show how intensely the reading failure matters to the parents of eleven-year-olds; but reassurance is vital. We can now quote to parents what has happened to pupils who have been working with us for five years. We can point out to them that the twenty-one worst readers in the school five years ago are now doing 136 CSE subject papers between them, and one or two O-levels: an average of six and a half subjects each. When those weak readers can succeed as well as this, our new crop of weak readers have also got a real hope of getting somewhere. Seven years of school failure already is not a guarantee of five more years of failure – given the right material, the right approach, and especially the right co-operation.

Of course, there are some pupils who are genuinely unintelligent, but who can tell for sure who they are? The effects of retardation in reading can be so acute that almost any form of intelligence test is likely to be affected. The Nelson Non-verbal Test has advantages here, and results from the E.P.V.T. or a professionally conducted W.I.S.C. can also be interesting. But there is a lot else besides intelligence that governs success. Parents may need some guidance on the question of intelligence. I find it helpful to speak of a child as being 'quite ordinary' or 'normal', in refuting the idea that he is seriously unintelligent. It is only a small minority of pupils receiving remedial help who are so unintelligent that they cannot achieve basic life-skills, reasonable reading, and even some CSE passes.

Another word that often needs to be discussed is 'dyslexia'. Parents get very worried about this term. Many parents of pupils who are only a little behind with their reading say 'Has he got dyslexia?', with that turn of phrase, and the anxious tone that would be suitable were they asking 'Has he got leukemia?'. There are many reasons why pupils become behind at reading – the next chapter considers some of them, but in my opinion dyslexia has not been a problem among any of the thousands of pupils I have taught up to this time. I suspect that the term is often harmful, in distracting attention from the real reasons for the lack of progress: certainly parents are scared of it, and pupils who hear they have 'got it' give up and despair of ever learning to read.

Discussions with parents then often move on to sibling rivalry. One often hears that a younger brother or sister can read better than Johnny. Parents are in a quandary: do they encourage the younger one, and praise him for what he can do, at the risk of discouraging the remedial pupil, or do they play down the success of the younger while boosting the morale of the elder? What can one recommend? Surely the younger must receive all the encouragement possible: his chances must not be jeopardized too. The only hope seems to lie in separation: try not to let them be too much aware of what the other can, or can not, do.

The parents' favourite books often loom large in discussions. 'I've got masses of books at home that I used to read, but he never looks at them.' The parent is hurt and disappointed that books that entertained him or her (before the age of television or lavish colour illustrations) do not seem to appeal to the child. The reading level is probably quite unsuitable anyway; and perhaps the parent was in fact thirteen or fourteen before he read *Treasure Island*, not eleven as he now imagines? And anyway, isn't there something about a book that has always been on the shelf as long as one can remember that makes it somehow a little less appealing than a new one? Finally, do the parents set an example here, sitting and quietly reading these books in front of the children? Actions count louder than words, and example is its own teacher.

It may also be necessary to discuss arrangements about an eye test or a hearing test; it is worth going through the details about how to get an eye test, as parents who have not had glasses themselves may not know. If the pupil is cross-lateral it is helpful to discuss the ways in which the parents can help in the training of a sense of left and right laterality – frequent use of the words 'left' and 'right', such as 'Can you pass me the salt? It's just to your left'; or asking the time 'Is it five to four or five past?'; or kinaesthetic training, like screwing and unscrewing, or patterns along a line from left to right. It can also be profitable to sound out as far as one can about bed-times and sleeping conditions (disturbance, fresh air?) – many pupils are in fact so chronically tired that learning is at best only fifty per cent of its potential rate.

And then one comes to the key question of the evening: 'What can I do to help?' A quick decision has to be made in the light of the discussion that has taken place: is this parent likely to be the sort of parent that will only make things worse, or is an offer of help a chance not to be missed, a way of doubling the amount of work done, and giving the pupil so much encouragement that success is almost inevitable?

Parents often do not realize that just because they are parents they stand in a special relationship with their children, which no one else shares. If the pupil does not please the teacher, at the end of the day he can go home, leave school behind him, say nasty things about the teacher, or pretend he does not exist; that teacher is only a periodic irritation, like a mosquito that comes buzzing and biting and disappears and ceases to annoy until the next day when it re-appears. But the parent is security, home, permanence and the mirror in which one's self-awareness is focused. If you fail while reading to your parent, and you are blamed for it, called a fool and an idiot, unintelligent and a failure, or a disgrace to the family, then these words apply to your life, not just your reading; they are with you night and day, in home and out of it.

No parent should help his child with remedial work unless he realizes what a special position a parent holds. No parent should help his child with remedial work unless he realizes that his child will be tired after a school day; that if you go on for more than a few minutes, increasing fatigue will lead to increasing errors, and increasing discouragement, and ultimately to the erosion of all the good that has been achieved during the day; or that if you choose the wrong material and the wrong time you will do more harm than good. But there are parents who have close bonds with their children, and the judgment and intuition to know when to begin and when to stop, how to help and when to leave alone. There are other parents – probably rather more – who can make sure in a firm but friendly way that homework is done, and yet not interfere with the homework.

The best help the parent of a remedial pupil can give is to take a warm and positive interest in the child and his progress – not to try to take on the role of teacher, but to fulfil the role of parent. Interest in what has been done; praise for success, however small; love and support; a kind word on a bad day, a firm word on a silly day and a fond word on a happy day. Not a bribe: 'If you get a good report you can have a new bicycle'. (How good a report? Who decides? And what happens if the report is not quite good enough? And was teacher fair anyway?) But instead of this: 'Finished another book already! Well done! Here's 50p.' 'Done another workbook? Very nice! I *am* pleased with you.'

Before the parents go, it is also important to stress that contact with them should be frequent: that they can contact you at the school whenever they want to, and you will contact them when you want to; not just at a pre-arranged parents' evening, but at any time when it is in the child's interests that parents and teachers should meet, or have a quick word on the telephone.

6. How did they get behind?

It has been my experience that there is no one single reason why pupils come to the secondary school retarded in reading and other skills in literacy, but that their retardation stems from one or more of a whole host of different causes. Often the event or circumstance that has led to the retardation was short and might even seem relatively trivial to an adult. The reason it can assume such proportions for a child is that it starts a vicious circle.

As soon as a pupil has fallen behind in class, that pupil is going to need more attention from the teacher, and will be working more slowly than the rest of the class. A teacher faced with a large class may not have time or the skill to help this pupil while carrying out all the other demands of a wide curriculum. If enough help is not given, the pupil inevitably slips further behind, needing more extra help and working even slower in relation to the rest of the class. Almost always the teacher keeps the slow reader waiting a few minutes while she sets work for the rest of the class: precious time is lost each day, which becomes a substantial amount of time in the course of the term, and bad work habits can be established along with a low self-image – circumstances that may lead to further retardation.

It is possible to become so obsessed in looking at the causes of retardation that one does nothing to correct the backwardness itself; but at the other extreme one can gain an understanding of the difficulties that will help towards a solution if one can discover where they began. The answer therefore must be to strike a balance.

The following representative selection of pupils may throw some light on the sort of difficulties that have led to retardation. This list, however, must not be thought of as statistically significant in any way; not only are the cases not ranked in any particular order of priority, but also there may well be other common causes of retardation that have been omitted. A full list of causes, with all the minor subdivisions, would be as long as the list of pupils needing remedial help.

The difficulties discussed here fall into four main categories: administrative, physical, emotional and other factors. Further insight into typical difficulties can be gained from Ravenette's excellent book *Dimensions of Reading Difficulties* (Pergamon).

Administrative difficulties

Valerie was born in August, which made her the youngest
pupil in her class. But in a way she should not have been in
that class at all, because she was born three months
prematurely. If she had been born as a full-term baby, she
would have arrived in early November, and gone through
school a whole year later. As it was, not only was she the
youngest in the class, but also much the smallest. To add to
her difficulties, she was not allowed to begin at the infant
school until the summer term. Most of the rest of her class
had begun in September or January; they knew the ropes,
and were well ahead of her when she arrived in April.
Although she was the least fitted to spend a shorter time in
infant school, she did in fact have two terms less than most
of her class. If only we allowed pupils to begin school five
years after their due date of birth, Valerie would probably
never have been behind.

But Sharon was behind too; she was born full term in
August, but even so was still at a disadvantage starting
school in April. In fact more than half the pupils we give
remedial help to had a 'less than full' time in the infant
school; very few who have the full three years in infant
school need remedial help. In other countries pupils all begin
school on the same date, once a year. One wonders if they
have the same degree of problems with remedial work.

Nick was five when he started in September, but he did
not stay in his first school long. His parents moved after he
had been there a term and a half, and then they moved
again when he was seven, and several times after that; by
the time he came to secondary school he was starting in his
seventh school. What with the time it takes to settle in to a
new class, with a new teacher and new friends, quite apart
from fundamental differences in techniques and approaches,
it is not surprising that the children like Nick – many of
them from Forces families – slip a long way behind with
their schooling.

Physical difficulties

Tina does not read particularly badly, but she does not make
the progress one would expect. In particular, she does not
seem to grasp whole principles in class, or to remember
clearly the content of her lessons. Perhaps this did not show
up too badly in her junior school because of the nature of the
work, the projects and individualized learning methods. But

now that her teachers are trying to prepare her for public examinations they are becoming more and more disappointed with her. Her difficulty is that she is prone to 'partial absence seizures', otherwise known as 'petit mal', and no one had noticed this. The seizures were brief but frequent, and enough to destroy the continuity of the work she was studying. Her vagueness and forgetfulness was not her fault; it was merely that she was intermittently absent during many of her lessons. The experts tell us that up to two per cent of the population may be prone to these seizures, and many are undetected and untreated.

John, however, had a bigger problem. As a clear epileptic he was heavily drugged – taking sixteen tablets a day to control his condition. The effect of these drugs on his system was so great that he was never able to function fully; it was as if his best was 'half speed ahead'.

Mike was clearly a pupil of good intelligence; he could respond quickly in class, usually seeing the point of work being done before almost anyone else; he had a good vocabulary and no difficulty with reading. But he had great difficulty in doing any form of written work. His drawings were crude and immature, his writing scratchy, ungainly, badly laid out, and irregular, his spelling disorganized, inconsistent and hard to read. Physically he was always restless, to the extent of being a problem in class. When he was born, his mother had had a long and difficult labour. A prolonged labour can leave the baby short of oxygen, causing permanent damage to the young brain cells, while difficult deliveries can lead to physical damage to some parts of the brain. Mike, like thousands of others, was one of the pupils who became a remedial pupil in the labour ward.

Nigel always seemed to get the letters wrong when he was reading, particularly letters like r and t, or n and m. He had passed the screening test for eyesight in school, but when his parents took him to the optician it was found that he clearly needed to have reading glasses. Suddenly print became easier to see, and his reading progressed fast.

Neil's spelling was poor, particularly showing errors of intrusions and omissions, and although he could read simple passages quite well, he had a lot of difficulty with longer words. He made some errors on the R.N.I.D. hearing test cards, and several errors on the Swansea Phonic Test, but he passed his test with the audiometrician without any difficulty. It appeared that his problem was sheer lack of training in aural discrimination, which meant that although he was at a reading stage of over nine, he could not tell what vowel to use when spelling a word, and often invented ends that were not there. A short spell of individualized training with the tape recorder and a 1:1 approach on phonic analysis and synthesis (done in an ordinary remedial group), including some work on nonsense words comparable to those used in the Swansea test, soon established the correct pattern, and his work in all subjects improved out of recognition.

Brian showed all the standard symptoms of the cross-lateral pupil – he was always getting b and d mixed up, and read 'was' for 'saw' and so on. It was not surprising because he was indeed cross-lateral: he had a strong right eye, and a strong left hand. Specific training of directionality led to a greatly reduced tendency to invert, and laid the foundations for building up his reading from a very low starting level.

David on the other hand was a clear right-lateral: he had a strong right eye (dominant and controlling), strong right hand and right foot; and yet he too was showing the problems of cross-laterality, including inversions. The reason in his case was that he wrote with his left hand, although he was naturally right handed. Why? 'When I was in the infants I broke my right arm, so the teacher suggested I should use my left, and I have done so ever since.' It proved impossible to re-establish the use of the right arm now that he was twelve but luckily he could respond to conventional remedial work, and made reasonable progress, although he will go through life as an 'induced cross-lateral', with the difficulties that stem from it.

Darren suffers from chronic fatigue. It seems that he rarely goes to bed until near the end of all television broadcasting, and even when he is in bed, he shares his room with his brother and his hamster; the hamster is often very lively during the night, waking the boys up with his running around in the cage. I doubt, too, whether the air in the room would be very fresh. Naturally class offers a quieter haven for sleeping, rather than being a stimulating place for working.

Emotional difficulties

Simon was seven, and just beginning to read (a bit late, perhaps, but beginning at last) when his older brother suddenly died. The effect was traumatic, not just on Simon, but on the whole family, and for some years it was a very depressed and unhappy family. Simon made no further progress with his reading until just before he came to us. He arrived still not knowing all the alphabet, and not scoring on most reading tests. Once started, however, despite the handicap of working in a comprehensive school at this level of literacy, his progress has been steady, even if rather slow. He recently enjoyed reading ninety-three pages of 'Trend' books in just an hour.

Roger hates reading, although perhaps he hates it less intensely now than he did when he arrived. I was surprised when I found this eleven-year-old, just arrived a week before, telling me in so many words that he hated reading and did not want to learn. But his reaction was entirely natural: both at home and at school reading had always been associated with violence or disgrace; it had never been pleasurable. His father regularly hit him because of his reading failure, and withdrew everything that Roger enjoyed until he should learn to read, while at junior school his class teacher either arranged for him to be heard reading by other members of his own class (which he found particularly distasteful), or to join a younger class and read with them. Fortunately Roger's father agreed to allow us to take on all the reading instruction, and he withdrew all his sanctions, and I think this is why Roger can now read adequately, even if not enthusiastically. He has certainly become a good fifth year pupil, expected to get good grades in at least six subjects at CSE.

Jane's mother believes in helping her to learn to read. The process might be a little more successful if it were not that Jane's own reading age, at about ten, is probably now equal to, or better than, her mother's. But mother says 'We enjoy our little reading games, don't we?', and they do them night after night, twenty minutes on, ten minutes off, all evening long. Mother is a very domineering lady. After a while Jane began to develop epileptic type symptoms when being taught by lady teachers. We put that down to a transferred mother image, and have tried to arrange for her to be taught by men, where no difficulties arise.

Linda was a happy and successful eight-year-old when her class had a new teacher. The teacher was a competent teacher, experienced, kindly, interested, professional; except that she had one quirk – apparently there had to be a scape-goat in every class. Linda became the scape-goat. She was always in trouble, although she gave no cause for it. When she was in trouble she had to stand with her hands on her head. Then the teacher would say, 'Look, everyone, Linda's crying. Clap, everyone, clap, Linda's crying.' The alarming thing about this story is that it is not unique: there have been other teachers I have heard of that have picked on a few pupils in a similar way. Personal vendettas are probably more common in junior schools than the profession likes to admit. This school was not in Swindon.

The proportion of pupils in our area who come from homes that have broken at least once is high; how many more come from homes that are under stress is anyone's guess. The current vogue of a feckless attitude to family life is no kindness to the children who suffer. How much they suffer is hard to say, but many must be the focus of the quarrels, like Vincent, who chose to live with Dad and his step-mother after the divorce went through. His step-mother had no regard for what his natural mother had done for him, and was openly very critical – in the most strident terms. The implication was that it was his mother's bad handling of Vincent that had led to his father having to break away. Yet Vincent went to see his mother twice a week, and it was clear that she was doing her best to retain his favour and to justify her past. Without being in his shoes it is hard to know just how awful Vincent must have felt day after day; but it is not hard to see why his thoughts were often far away from his work. Luckily a counsellor was able to help here.

Other factors that lead to difficulties

Paula started school in an infants' school that used i.t.a. After about four terms she left and has not used i.t.a. again. But she finds reading discouraging, and in particular she finds spelling almost impossible; many of the i.t.a. variants still persist in her work. Whether or not i.t.a. is a good way of starting infants on their reading is a matter for the experts: but one does not have to be an expert to see the damaging effect of an *unfinished* course of i.t.a. – and we seem to have quite a few such pupils.

Bob is far behind with his work, and has little appetite for school things. He is a big youth, taller than most of his teachers, strong and mature. Spend a little while talking with him, and one will discover that before he comes to school in the morning he has to look after all the rest of the family, get them breakfast and off to school, clear up and make the beds. In the evening he is similarly responsible for the domestic chores, supper and clearing up. Every failure, real or imagined, is punished by father with a great deal of violence. School may be a haven, but school work is not exactly manna from heaven for a youth who is probably more mechanically than linguistically gifted anyway.

When Judy joined us, her father sent a rather aggressive letter saying that he would never allow her to do homework, and she was never to be kept in. When the head asked Father to come and discuss the matter, he only got a brief refusal. Father had something of a reputation for violence, so we were wondering what we were going to face when he did turn up for our special remedial parents' evening. Aggressive though he was at first, we allowed him to talk for a while. We then enquired gently how the girl herself felt about her homework. We reassured him that his daughter was not severely retarded, but nevertheless in need of some help. And then his story came out: how he had been in an overcrowded East End slum school, how they had tried to teach him Latin and calculus although he could not read and write, how often they caned him, and how often he was truant; how he had kept the secret of his illiteracy from the people at work and from his children, and how he feared that if his daughter came home with homework – and asked him for help, his own failure would suddenly be discovered. And the telling was its own cure. He withdrew his opposition; Judy regularly takes homework home, and he always comes to school for parents' evenings or if staff want to see him.

Henry moved into his junior school in the third year (aged ten), from another district, almost unable to read. The peripatetic remedial teacher said that he was 'too weak' to have remedial help; his group was full of other pupils having help, and there was no time for Henry. So Henry was put in a corner of the classroom, along with some other backward readers, and spent much of the time drawing – or playing the fool. My conclusion at the end of the diagnostic period was that Henry couldn't read because no one had ever taught him how to. Given a good stiff straight programme of instruction, within six months he was already years ahead in reading age.

Chris was a weak reader, but not too bad at 'making the right noises' when he saw print – it was just that he did not always understand what he read. But then there were so few words that he did really understand. Like Bob, he was the home-help, and his life was contained between home, the local shops, and school; hardly ever did he venture beyond. When he was asked what the 'sea' was, he named the local lake. The same was true of so many other basic nouns that it was clear that his thinking had not yet developed to a level at which he could profit from, say, television, still less from school. Before much progress with reading was possible, he needed a great deal of conceptual development.

Tom seems English enough if you see him in class, working quietly and hard in his school uniform; there is little in his features to suggest anything else. He is making good progress, and can read well now, although he hardly managed anything when he arrived. But he still has difficulty with vocabulary and meaning – which is not really surprising since the only English he speaks is at school. His parents are Turkish, and at home he speaks nothing but Turkish.

One factor that has not been mentioned is intelligence. I do not think that any of the pupils referred to here have been impeded in their reading development by lack of intelligence. Some of the pupils are bright, some are not so bright; but, had they had good opportunities for learning to read, and had the factors mentioned here been removed, I believe they would all have reached an adequate reading level before they came to our school.

7. Teaching literacy to all the pupils in the secondary school

It would not seem to be unreasonable to assume that to advance one's reading stage from 12.0 to 13.0 it is likely, for most pupils, to involve a fair degree of reading, and more still is likely to be needed to reach a reading stage of 14.0. If this is so, it is of interest to find out how much time pupils actually spend on reading in the course of a school week, and what sort of reading it is that they are doing. Similar comments can be made for written work, including handwriting, spelling and the more advanced skills such as paragraphing.

In a survey by a number of colleagues, three different ways of estimating the time spent on reading by a typical first-year pupil all produced the figure of eleven per cent. Although this figure is subjective rather than scientific, the fact that the different ways of calculating it produced the same answer does suggest that it is not too far from the truth. What is more, it seems that most of the eleven per cent was made up of small bits of reading, rather than any extended reading, and that the reading concerned was 'occasional' rather than programmed. The amount of time spent on written work was not quite so precisely calculated, but was slightly more than the time spent on reading.

Have we any right to assume that a normal eleven-year-old or twelve-year-old will indeed progress at a normal rate in reading, and develop the higher order reading skills, as advocated in the Bullock Report, without a planned programme of literacy development? Some English Departments will probably answer that they do in fact provide such a programme, and if they do the pupils will be well served. But it is likely that in many secondary schools there is, as the Bullock Committee feared, little by way of a planned programme of literacy development. The English Department may well say (and with good cause), that their role is in literature and drama, in creative work and the development of personality, in vicarious experience and artistic expression; that these are important areas, and occupy all the time that is available. Other departments are likely to argue that they are there for teaching their own specialist subjects, and that they have not got the time to stop and teach skimming, scanning, the use of an index, paragraphing, punctuation, and so on. And if the matter is left there, no systematic teaching occurs. Pupils who enter the secondary school above the level considered to need remedial help, get no help from anyone.

The answer is not simple. It is not good enough just to decree that these matters shall be the concern of every department, that everyone shall make it his or her concern to ensure that the pupils read a lot and write a lot every week, and that they teach the higher order reading skills. For one thing, some teachers are so little interested in these areas that they would not handle them well. Secondly, if the work is not properly graded, it might well be injurious, at any rate to the weaker readers. Thirdly, reading is not the only skill that needs to be considered. There is also the development of vocabulary, the extension of general knowledge, and the teaching of certain learning skills.

Mention has been made in an earlier chapter of the fact that inadequate vocabulary often proves a stumbling block for moderately proficient readers, such as those at a reading stage of around 10.0. There is a lot of vocabulary that secondary school teachers consider is basic knowledge in their subjects, but they often do not specifically explain it. At a conference discussing the Bullock Report, a list of nearly two hundred technical terms felt to be necessary in school for first-year pupils was quickly drawn up – an average of ten or twenty from each main department. Many pupils probably spend much of their day half understanding words that have never been properly explained to them. At times they may well misunderstand. Not only are the words not explained, but as often as not no one has shown the pupils how to find out what the words do mean, or stimulated them to take an interest in enlarging their vocabulary.

The transfer to secondary school may well also involve transfer to teachers who glibly tell a class to 'learn this by heart', or 'revise this term's work', without ever explaining to the pupils how they can most efficiently commit something to memory, or set about doing revision. Learning skills of this sort are best discussed, taught and practised. Every pupil's learning ability can be improved by attention to these things.

It is surprising how little general knowledge may be known by a modern eleven-year-old, although which gaps are most blatant must surely vary from school to school, depending on the emphases of the different lessons in each school. Pupils may not be able to identify the major continents and countries of the world on outline maps, or may not know what a planet is, or about the development of the machine age, or about proverbs, sayings and folk lore. Some of these things are more important than others, but when they are all lacking we have a pupil who is not properly educated in the traditional culture of our nation. Some attention to the acquisition of general knowledge, as appropriate for each school, needs to be considered as part of the basic training in literacy.

Finally, there is the 'service' element of English teaching; the need to teach formal English so that it can be used when teaching other subjects. Once again the exact needs will vary from school to school, but they are likely to include the teaching of spelling rules, practice in spelling corrections, knowledge of all the main punctuation rules, some knowledge at least of nouns, verbs, and adjectives, and work on paragraphing. All this may be covered in the English lessons, but if it is not, a place must be found elsewhere.

In our case, the remedial teachers also teach a subject called 'General Studies'. Classes throughout the first and second years are given two lessons a week which cover the sort of material that has been outlined in this chapter. Besides the points already mentioned, the course includes work on how to use a dictionary, on how to set out work, and specific worksheets on other such areas, which train a variety of skills in short projects lasting one or two weeks.

If the course manages to awaken an interest in vocabulary, to maintain and develop work from the junior school on presentation, tidiness, accuracy and precision, and to introduce learning techniques suitable for the secondary school, it is helping to ensure that pupils who enter the school not needing help, do continue not to need it.

8. The older pupils

Pupils in the last two years of secondary school need a different approach from the younger pupils. Whereas the first or second-year pupil will work hard to please teacher, and therefore only needs to like the teacher to be well motivated, the older pupil sees himself as an adult, and wants to be treated as an adult – although he is often very insecure, and ill-equipped to behave like one.

We run two courses for the less-proficient fourth and fifth-year pupils: one is called 'Basic Skills', and the other is an English lesson. Both attempt to develop literacy in the broadest sense, and the ability to cope with the adult world. (Further details on both these courses are given below.)

We also give help to pupils of this age who are still finding spelling difficult even though they seem to be able to cope with the rest of their school work satisfactorily. The workbook *Do-it-Yourself Spelling* has been prepared particularly with these pupils in mind.

There does not seem to be any point in presenting these young adults with the limited vocabulary, stilted phrases, and phonic schemes that are traditionally used with younger pupils. Reading is much more difficult if you are not interested in what it is about. These pupils do not want trivial material; they want material that challenges them, that treats them as young citizens, and that is varied.

It is true that if the reading level of the material we use on these courses is assessed on a reading-level formula, it will appear to be far ahead of the level they have reached. But this only goes to show the inadequacy of the formula, because they can, with a certain amount of help, read what we ask them to read. Presumably they achieve this partly through a look-and-say approach, and partly by using contextual clues, to boost what they can achieve from the phonic and word-building approaches.

In both courses we find that vocabulary is once again very much a clue to reading ability. The stumbling block is often not the actual decoding of the printed word, but knowing and understanding the word itself. This is why it is so important that these pupils should do work at school on these areas, under the guidance of a teacher.

Some of the pupils doing these courses are still very far behind with their reading. They may well have struggled for some years on remedial work in the junior school, and not prospered on our individualized programmes either; we do have a small number who reach the fourth year still extremely weak – perhaps about five pupils in a year group of about three hundred. We still use the same material with these pupils, although they may well need individual help to go through it word by word, and progress may be slow. Yet they benefit, because they seem to rise to the challenge the material offers. I have not yet known any of these pupils to seize-up at the sight of the material presented in either Basic Skills or the English class.

Basic Skills

The Basic Skills course is run as an option in our school, along with other fourth year options. Careful work in the third year, chiefly done by the tutors, ensures that the right pupils opt for this course. No persuasion is used, but care is taken to make quite sure that the less able pupils appreciate what is in the course, and what the work will be like; usually they are keen to do it as soon as they have understood what is entailed. Occasionally one of the pupils – perhaps misled at home – opts for a much too academic course. When this happens the tutors need to explain what the academic study of, say, Chemistry, involves, and to contrast this with what Basic Skills covers. We are careful also to ensure that Basic Skills is presented as a mixed-ability option. We find in practice that the pupils themselves are the best judges of who would benefit most from doing Basic Skills, and they are not always the same as those who need help with reading. We explain that the way to decide whether to do the course or not, is to look through the list of skills covered, and to ask oneself, 'Could I do these things without asking anyone how to do it?' If the answer is no, then the pupil should opt for the course.

In the four years that the course has been offered as an option, the number taking it has been rising gradually, so that now just over one in six of the year group opt for it. A Mode 3 CSE paper in 'General Studies' (not to be confused with the different subject taught in years one and two), ensures that pupils do not 'miss out' on the chance of a CSE by taking this option.

A wide range of skills is covered, and these are often grouped into themes that run for a month or two. Full details of possible groupings are given in the teacher's notes at the back of the book, *Basic Skills You Need*. The range of

skills covered in this book are summarized here, but in fact
we also cover various other skills and aspects of general
knowledge not contained in the book. The companion book,
Practice in Basic Skills, gives additional work on each of the
same skills.

Abbreviations
Checking a bicycle or a car
Coping in the kitchen
Reading sales literature
Gardening
Money sums
Simple nursing
Filling in forms, and an income tax form
Getting discounts
Getting foreign money
Finding out by phone
Going on holiday
Handling timetables
The country we live in
Europe
The Highway Code
Trade unions
Lay-out
Locating in alphabetical order
Looking things up
Making sense of percentages
Voting
Punctuation
Reading instructions
The 24-hour clock
Reading to children
Giving directions
Interviews
Visit the doctor
Handwriting
Common weights and measures
The weather forecast
Using a dictionary
Using banks and cheques
Wiring three-pin plugs
Writing a business letter

A pupil who has worked through the literacy elements of

this list of 'Basic Skills' is reasonably well qualified to take his place in the adult world.

Fourth and fifth year English

The book *English You Need*, with its associated anthology *Need a Read?*, is intended for use with small or large classes of fourth and fifth-year pupils both in the non-examination and the CSE groups. It is a course designed to lead to the usual CSE English Language paper, for those pupils who have the ability to reach the required standard.

The book tries to grasp the nettles firmly – it deals with basic phonics, reading speeds, simple and more extensive spelling problems, the use of a dictionary and punctuation rules. Every chapter contains several sections that have straight-forward reading; every chapter has a 'word-match' section to develop vocabulary, and a crossword which presents an opportunity to recapitulate on some of the harder words of the chapter.

Every chapter also has a section called 'controversy', with five provocative ideas, which can be used for debates, class discussion, or talking points. Many of the other sections in each chapter can also be taken orally if the teacher feels the pupils will do themselves more justice this way.

There is no justification for assuming that a pupil who finds fluent reading or exact written work difficult should be debarred from discussing the aspects of adult life, employment, social reform or recreation that many of his peers are discussing. Nor is there any need to bow to the current vogue of concentrating on sordid, vulgar, or depressing social evils. An important feature of this book is the consistent policy of boosting these pupils' morale: not what they cannot do, but what they can; not 'down to their level', but 'up to their potential'.

But English teaching requires literature to feed on; and it is assumed that the class teacher will be bearing this in mind. The companion volume *Need a Read?* brings together a wide selection of literature arranged to run in parallel with the chapters of *English You Need*.

Need a Read? contains twenty-four short pieces that represent almost as many distinct forms of literature, and it is hoped that pupils will come to realize that some of these forms have a special appeal for them, and therefore will want to look further at these types.

Although both these courses are conceived primarily as

ones for teaching a group of pupils largely together, we also try to maintain an element of individualization. A special record card for use with fourth and fifth-year pupils aims to identify the areas where the particular pupil needs most individual help so that these areas can be highlighted. Within a group, all the pupils are likely to be working on the same general theme at the same time; but they do not all need to be working on the same tasks within that theme, but rather to concentrate on those that are most relevant to themselves.

9. Organization

When considering a method for teaching literacy in the secondary school, particularly for remedial work in smaller groups, one must take into account all aspects of organization, including the deployment of staff. Pressures on schools are so great that it is essential that everyone should be employed as effectively as possible, and it is reasonable that those in responsibility should be able to ask what results are achieved from the employment of each individual teacher.

Many schools like to set aside a small group of pupils in some form of remedial unit. Pupils who are divided off in this way may find it very difficult ever to get back into the ordinary class. Another point is that a remedial unit is rather wasteful of staff. A small number of pupils benefit all day long from these specially trained staff while all the other pupils in the school receive no benefit from these teachers at all. One can even ask who is best qualified to teach the retarded pupils their Science, History, Drama, or Home Studies. Is it the remedial specialist or the subject specialist? Do the pupils always benefit from being in a group where everyone has difficulties? Could they benefit at all from being in a group where some do not have the same difficulties?

If the pupils who have difficulties are included in a mixed-ability class it will be necessary to withdraw them from class for special help. This, it is commonly argued, only puts them further behind. But the truth is that in an ideal world no pupils would reach the secondary school so seriously behind with reading as to need special help. It is therefore an unsatisfactory situation when such a pupil arrives in the secondary school, and any solution will have some unsatisfactory element also. To miss one lesson a week of a particular subject is a relatively small price to pay, and if the reward is progress in reading, it is an investment that pays off well.

My policy is to withdraw each pupil for one lesson a day if a lot of work has to be done, but for only two or three lessons a week if the programme is not so full. I try to ensure that no one subject loses more than one lesson a week, and a timetable is set up in consultation with the pupil. This does not mean that the pupil has licence to avoid all the lessons he dislikes, but it does mean that if a pupil has, say, a special talent at drama, he is not withdrawn from the drama lesson. If one were to withdraw a pupil from more than one lesson a week of a particular subject, as a normal rule it would be tantamount to condemning him to failure in that subject.

When a pupil is in a withdrawal group, he is missing a lesson by a skilled subject teacher. It may well be a very good lesson, by a very good teacher. It follows therefore that the withdrawal lesson must be so good, and so exactly what the pupil needs, that it is of more value than the lesson missed. To ensure that this happens the withdrawal group must be small enough to allow the teacher to give enough personal attention and coaching to justify having that pupil there. To have six pupils present at a time, for a lesson of thirty-five or forty minutes, is the maximum possible on this method. Six pupils means six individual programmes, and is like having six classes at the same time. This allows five minutes of individual coaching per lesson, and, with suitably programmed work, this should give the basis for really fast progress.

In fact when a withdrawal group is timetabled for five periods a week, one is not restricted to a total of six pupils within it. I prefer this type of group to have about nine pupils: three who really have serious problems and need to come every day, and about six more who can come two or three times a week, turn and turn about, so that all nine pupils never come together at the same time. In this way six withdrawal groups can cope with a total of fifty-four pupils being withdrawn.

Many heads like to use sixth formers to help with hearing reading. A secondary pupil who is having difficulty with reading has not managed to learn to read despite the efforts of about seven junior school class teachers (several of whom were probably very good), and quite possibly one or two specially trained primary remedial teachers. Why then is there so much hope that an untrained pupil, just five years older than the remedial pupil, should be able to manage what the trained teachers cannot? Certainly hearing reading is not a passive matter; effective hearing of reading is a dynamic process, which requires a deep understanding of the reading process and the problems facing a learner. The whole of this manual has also emphasized that hearing reading should be at most a very small part of the remedial work. If sixth formers have time to help, why cannot they take the straight classroom lessons, firmly structured on clear textbooks, in subjects they know and understand well, and release those teachers to help the pupils who need the most skilled teaching of all?

Similar comments must apply to the help of parents. The chapter on the role of parents discussed the problem of knowing which parents are capable of helping their own children best. The problem is just as acute about knowing which parents can help their next door neighbours' children. It is a big risk to take a parent on in this way.

Our groups in years three, four and five (and also some sixth form groups) are somewhat larger, because we are not using the same degree of prescriptive teaching at these levels – it is therefore possible to run up to ratios of 12:1 or 15:1. To run a group larger than this however becomes ineffective; not enough help can be given to each pupil to justify arranging the course at all.

The General Studies classes however are full classes, usually of twenty-nine or thirty pupils in mixed-ability groups.

There is no point trying to do remedial work with the first and second-year pupils without beginning with diagnostic work, and time must be found for this. But since the beginning and end of withdrawal lessons does not need to coincide with the beginning and end of any term, the amount of time used for diagnostic work can vary at different times of the year. In the early autumn a lot of lessons will be needed for diagnostic work, but once the new entrants have been seen, it is possible to set up one or two extra learning groups in some of the time taken by the diagnostic periods, retaining the other periods for follow-up work on pupils working through their programmes.

Remedial teaching is very demanding and exhausting, and at times can be discouraging. Where it is successful, it brings new hope and new chances. Every secondary school head has a responsibility for seeing that the pupils and the staff in his school have the best facilities he can provide, and are organized in the way that best suits the school.

10. The sense of achievement through the Dorcan Scheme

The Dorcan Scheme is designed to help teachers to encourage their pupils through a sense of achievement, and to let the pupils get some fun from their learning. We think it is important that teachers should exploit that aspect to the full. Everyone needs a sense of achievement in learning.

Many teachers, when they were pupils, got this sense of achievement for themselves by being the successful ones in the school, gaining the higher marks in examinations, the higher positions in class order, or being placed in the higher streams. We should never forget how much the signs of success and approval helped most of us while we were at school – the knowledge that we could almost always do the work well, get a good comment, and obtain the teachers' and our parents' approval.

Contrast this with the learning situation for a twelve, thirteen or fourteen-year-old who is a long way behind with reading. Chapter Six of this manual gives the case histories of about twenty typical pupils who were behind through no fault of their own. They were not behind because they had not got the intelligence to be further forward; they were behind through factors that they could see and understand, but not influence. Having a fair degree of intelligence they can fully appreciate the failure, and the success the others enjoy. They know how much they are behind, and this only makes their position more intolerable.

Some, of course, are 'below average' in general intelligence in so far as such a thing exists – but let us not deceive ourselves: an I.Q. even as low as 80 means a twelve-year-old has a 'mental age' of 9.6, and a normal child of nine-and-a-half is very well aware of the world around him. Most of our pupils are brighter than this, whatever their reading age may be.

Hence the diagnostic and prescriptive approach of the Dorcan Scheme is not just a matter of the wise use of resources: it is a vital element in the underlying philosophy of encouraging the pupil. Unfortunately much of the old traditional remedial work insults our pupils. To offer trite fiction in a 'controlled vocabulary' and then to take turns in reading it aloud is insulting. To print in large type and illustrate with simplified drawings is insulting. To offer material that was prepared for much younger pupils is insulting.

There is a danger that many tasks set for pupils who are far behind in reading can also be insulting. They can be so obvious, or so condescending, that no satisfaction is gained from doing them.

But there is another huge problem facing the teacher when the pupil is far behind with reading – how does one prevent the task ahead from seeming too daunting? One can make fast progress with reading, but it is not possible to avoid the rungs on the ladder, and there are a lot of rungs between a very low reading score and efficient adult reading. A teacher who attempts to encourage a pupil by suggesting that the way ahead is easy is misleading the pupil. What perhaps is meant, and what can certainly be done, is to make the way ahead as easy as possible by the careful use of the right material.

This is what the individual programme can achieve, and it is vital that teachers using the scheme should familiarize themselves with the ideas behind the workbooks, as discussed in Chapter Two, and the ways of setting up and modifying a programme, as discussed in Chapter Three. In the same way it is vital that the school organization should be such that they can fit in diagnostic work, and run reading groups that have individual programmes, as discussed in Chapter Nine. If it is appropriate to continue and consolidate the work on literacy with fifteen and sixteen-year-old pupils using the books *Basic Skills you Need, Practice in Basic Skills, English You Need,* and *Need a Read?,* as discussed in Chapter Eight, the organization should allow for this too.

With programmes and organization established correctly, it should be possible to build the pupils' confidence and sense of achievement. There should be fun in a reading group. The teacher's and the pupils' approach to the work should be optimistic and responsive. There should be a quiet, busy, businesslike atmosphere – not the silence of convicts sentenced to dreary punishments.

There should be a sense of achievement built up in many ways. There should be the achievement of pages completed. Each workbook has varied tasks, and the tasks are usually short enough and self-contained enough to be completed in something between a quarter and half-an-hour. Each source book is not very long, and the section of work on it is not excessively long either, so it should be possible to complete several source books ('rungs on the ladder'), and the workbooks that go with them, in the course of a term. Every such task completed should be seen as another achievement, and the pupils should gain the same reward and satisfaction as we used to, when, as pupils, we did well in an examination, or were well placed in the form order.

Then there should be the sense of achievement from learning useful things: from knowing more facts about skateboards or Scandinavia, dinosaurs or diet, birds or Britain. The material the pupils are asked to read is valuable in itself: it is worthy of their attention – and it should help build up their confidence in themselves, their image of themselves as normal teenagers, and their standing among their peers. Teachers should not just use source books and workbooks as wordbanks; they should discuss and develop the interest of the material presented, as well as the words used.

There should be a sense of achievement from the tasks undertaken. There should be satisfaction from knowing the alphabet backwards and forwards, from being able to read Morse Code, from touch typing, from being able to do a crossword, solve an anagram, find a rhyme; from improved spelling, careful handwriting, and most of all from the self-awareness built up through the discussions over the Challenge book.

You can lead a horse to water but you can't make him drink. You can saturate a weak reader with phonics and sight vocabulary, assignments and graded material, and he will still learn nothing. You can teach hard all day, and the pupils still learn nothing. Learning is such a personal thing, that co-operation, confidence and involvement are essential factors. The Dorcan Scheme is designed for the use of teachers who are going to exploit these approaches, and it will be most successful in the hands of teachers who do not just follow the scheme mechanically, but also enter the spirit of the approach involved.

Appendices

Appendix 1 Dorcan Spelling Analysis. Questions for test list DSA-01

Please speak clearly and adhere exactly to the list and cue sentences.

1	Hit.	The car hit a lamp post. Hit.
2	Wet.	Sometimes we have a very wet day. Wet.
3	Jam.	I like lots of jam on my bread. Jam.
4	Lid.	You can put a lid on a saucepan while you cook. Lid.
5	Cup.	I drink my tea out of a cup. Cup.
6	Son.	A boy is his father's son. Son.
7	Ivy.	Ivy is a green plant that climbs up trees. Ivy.
8	Rock.	The ship hit a rock and sank. Rock.
9	Beg.	Some people teach their dogs to sit up and beg. Beg.
10	Fix.	You must fix a hook in the wall before you hang the picture up. Fix.
11	Date.	A calendar tells you what the date is. Date.
12	When.	A timetable tells you when the bus goes. When.
13	Side.	The home side did well at the football match. Side.
14	Go.	When the bell rings for the end of school we go home. Go.
15	Hope.	The school team had little hope of winning. Hope.
16	Ship.	A ship goes across the ocean. Ship.
17	Thin.	If you don't eat enough you will be too thin. Thin.
18	Tune.	You can play a good tune with a recorder. Tune.
19	Baker.	A baker's job is to make bread. Baker.
20	These.	These are the buns you ordered. These.
21	High.	Snowdon is quite a high mountain. High.
22	Chop.	A butcher has to chop the meat. Chop.
23	For.	We have bread and butter for tea. For.
24	Saw.	They saw the moon come up over the trees. Saw.
25	Strong.	A farmer has to be very strong. Strong.
26	Here.	Come here, doggy! Good dog! Here.
27	Quick.	You have to be quick to get the ball in a good game. Quick.
28	Phone.	More and more people are having the phone at home. Phone.
29	Great.	Most people think their favourite groups are great. Great.
30	One.	One and one make two. One.
31	Toy.	All children like to have a toy to play with. Toy.
32	Food.	Some people like too much food to eat. Food.
33	Rain.	We get lots of rain in Britain. Rain.
34	Seem.	You seem to be working hard. Seem.
35	Loud.	The noise was too loud and the teacher was cross. Loud.
36	Foam.	Firemen spray foam on some fires. Foam.
37	Beak.	A bird has to pick things up with its beak. Beak.
38	Boil.	We boil the water before we make the tea. Boil.
39	Head.	One's head is very strong. Head.
40	Brief.	There was a brief pause in the game. Brief.
41	Age.	The age for having a vote is eighteen. Age.
42	Price.	Shops mark the price of their goods. Price.
43	Station.	You catch the train at the station. Station.
44	Fight.	You must not fight in school. Fight.
45	Kindly.	Could you kindly show me the way? Kindly.
46	Flies.	A plane flies very fast. Flies.
47	Circle.	You can draw a circle with a compass. Circle.
48	Netted.	The centre forward netted the ball. Netted.
49	Playful.	Kittens are usually very playful. Playful.
50	Driving.	He lost his driving licence for speeding. Driving.

Dorcan Spelling Analysis.
Questions for test list DSA-02

Please speak clearly and adhere exactly to the list and cue sentences.

1	Din.	Teachers do not like to hear a loud din. Din.
2	Vet.	If an animal is ill we take him to the vet. Vet.
3	Sack.	If you work badly you will get the sack. Sack.
4	Lip.	She bit her lip because she was upset. Lip.
5	Mud.	After hard rain there is a lot of mud around. Mud.
6	Ton.	A bike does a ton at a hundred miles an hour. Ton.
7	Happy.	He smiles when he is happy. Happy.
8	Can.	The Americans call a tin a can. Can.
9	Rub.	People used to rub two sticks together to make fire. Rub.
10	Fox.	A fox has a big bushy tail. Fox.
11	Tape.	You can measure things with a tape. Tape.
12	Why.	I wonder why you did this? Why.
13	Rise.	It is nice to see the sun rise. Rise.
14	So.	It was a nice day so I went out. So.
15	Note.	I left a note for the milkman before I went. Note.
16	Wish.	I wish it would be nice every day. Wish.
17	Moth.	I saw a moth settle on my jumper so I killed it. Moth.
18	June.	The month after May is June. June.
19	Taken.	The thief has taken all my jewels. Taken.
20	Even.	Even though the thief left fingerprints the police couldn't find him. Even.
21	Sigh.	It was so disappointing I had to sigh. Sigh.
22	Chart.	A chart is a sort of map. Chart.
23	Scorn.	He was full of scorn when he saw my work. Scorn.
24	Paw.	Our dog hurt his paw on some broken glass. Paw.
25	String.	String is useful for tying parcels. String.
26	Pear.	A pear is a bit like an apple. Pear.
27	Quite.	Your work is quite good most of the time. Quite.
28	Photo.	I took a photo of the sunrise when I went out. Photo.
29	Eight.	Four and four make eight. Eight.
30	None.	None of these make much sense. None.
31	Joy.	The dog bounded with joy when his master came home. Joy.
32	Foot.	I didn't hurt my foot because I had my shoes on. Foot.
33	Raid.	The bandits made a raid on the bank. Raid.
34	Meet.	I said I would meet her at half past four. Meet.
35	Pound.	There are a hundred pennies in one pound. Pound.
36	Road.	They are building a new road out of our town. Road.
37	Leak.	There is a leak in the roof where the rain gets in. Leak.
38	Soil.	The soil in our garden is no good. Soil.
39	Dead.	Our cat brought a dead bird into the kitchen. Dead.
40	Thief.	The police got the thief in the end. Thief.
41	Cage.	Our parrot does not like his cage. Cage.
42	Twice.	You've been told twice how to do it. Twice.
43	Pension.	At the age of sixty-five everyone can have a pension. Pension.
44	Right.	Turn left, turn right, and right again. Right.
45	Spies.	The government uses spies to find out secrets. Spies.
46	Windy.	When it is windy branches fall off trees. Windy.
47	Purple.	Purple clothes are very popular. Purple.
48	Rotted.	The apple rotted in the corner. Rotted.
49	Hopeful.	The team were hopeful of winning. Hopeful.
50	Living.	The cost of living keeps on going up. Living.

Dorcan Spelling Analysis DSA-01

Key word	Reversals	Homophones*	Correct phonic structure
1 Hit			
2 Wet	Met		whet wett weat
3 Jam	Lam jam		
4 Lid	libe leb lib		
5 Cup	cub		
6 Son		sun	
7 Ivy	vie iev viey		ivey eyeve ivea
8 Rock	rak		rok
9 Beg			beag
10 Fix	fisk fisc		fiks ficks fics
11 Date	Gate bate deat		dayt
12 When	Met		wen
13 Side	seid sibe sib	sighod	
14 Go			gow goe
15 Hope	hobe hape		
16 Ship			
17 Thin			
18 Tune			chuen choon chewn
19 Baker	dacker bacri bark		baekur baeker
20 These			theas thees thease
21 High		hi	hie hiye hiy huy hiey hy
22 Chop			
23 For		four fore	
24 Saw	was	sore soar	soor sor
25 Strong			
26 Here		hear	heaer heer

* It is assumed that the following words are outside the pupils' vocabulary and therefore do not count as homophones – whet wen hie

Some sample answers to aid analysis

Wrong symbol	Intrusions	Omissions	Non-phonic	Key word	
het hite ite	hits			Hit	1
wat wete				Wet	2
jim jame				Jam	3
lide led lad lede leat lead				Lid	4
cap				Cup	5
sune				Son	6
ive ivei iviife ifey iveye ieve	iver ivel live		iav	Ivy	7
rook roak rooke			rore	Rock	8
bege beck baeg back bag beak	berk		beap	Beg	9
thix fick thicks fikes fecks fiss	fings fiexs fixs fist		fegse	Fix	10
dat dit	datl			Date	11
wan wene wem wean	went		were	When	12
sid sayd	sind shid		said	Side	13
				Go	14
hop hoop holp	holp			Hope	15
shic sep shipe	sipet			Ship	16
fin thine fein	fingun			Thin	17
tuon chun tchun tun terne chone tuone	trun		tshon thon chon	Tune	18
backer bacer bekr	barkey	bake	beace	Baker	19
thes theys vecs	theirs theses		ther	These	20
hugh hiue hoy haiy	hight hite hire			High	21
cop shop cope jop shope thop	copper chorp			Chop	22
			foys fove	For	23
soy sow sour suw	sawer salt		sae	Saw	24
stronge stron strog srong		stong trong stog		Strong	25
hare hire her heve				Here	26

Dorcan Spelling Analysis DSA-01

Key word	Reversals	Homophones*	Correct phonic structure
27 Quick	ɒiɒ		cwik quik cwick kwick qwiq
28 Phone	tone		fone fown phown
29 Great	gart	grate	
30 One		won	
31 Toy			
32 Food	thob		
33 Rain	rian	rein reign	rane raen raine
34 Seem		seam	seme seym
35 Loud	laed lawd		lowd lowed
36 Foam	tome foow		fome fowm foem
37 Beak	deack deck deke bekc		beke beack beeck
38 Boil	biol dole doyul boli		boyoll boyall boyol boile boill boiyl
39 Head	haed heab heb		hed
40 Brief	dreaf dreth daef derf brife		breaf brefe breef
41 Age	aje		aje
42 Price			
43 Station	stastion sastoin staitoin		stashun staysen stashon
44 Fight			fite fiet
45 Kindly			kindley kindlee
46 Flies	fyls files	fly's	flise flys
47 Circle			surkoll surcol sercol circul
48 Netted			
49 Playful	aplyth palyall		playfull plafull
50 Driving	divering bife brivig diring biv		driveing

Some sample answers to aid analysis

Wrong symbol	Intrusions	Omissions	Non-phonic	Key word	
qicke quck cike cwek quike qike qick	quink		gike kike	Quick	27
thone pone fon thwon fohen	throne four font ponen		thopon	Phone	28
grat grite greate	geest	gate geet	graght	Great	29
			oum	One	30
top tor toye	torn			Toy	31
foude fowd	footd		fone	Food	32
ran	rai		lay	Rain	33
sime sem seim seen sen seeim sam	semd			Seem	34
lad larde lod lade	louid		lawed loghd	Loud	35
foom fom foan foum phom			thoume fomr	Foam	36
bech beik beck beick back beg bike bek	barck		bag	Beak	37
bole bil bowl baill bool boel boul	boral borud borle		booly bolle	Boil	38
hede had	herd		hond	Head	39
breth bref blef brev brith breath brif		befe bief	bado brige	Brief	40
ag eaje	gaj		arsh	Age	41
prize pric pris prise prase	privice	pice pis	plces	Price	42
stasun shasun stahon		stion staion	sam	Station	43
fit fute fiht	frit			Fight	44
condle cindiy	kindler	kidlie kinly	ciy kiper	Kindly	45
flis flese fles		fis fiys fly	flic fling	Flies	46
serkole sukel circil		cirle	socal cucol	Circle	47
netid netide neted kneted netit	netded nened netter	nete	nedy	Netted	48
playfal playfell plofel pliyfull	playfor	play pafal	palyt	Playful	49
drivin drivig	drivering driven	diving diven diveing dirve	joi	Driving	50

Dorcan Spelling Analysis DSA-02

Key word	Reversals	Homophones*	Correct phonic structure
1 Din	bin		dinn
2 Yet			
3 Sack			sak sac
4 Lip	lib		
5 Mud	mub		
6 Ton			tun
7 Happy			
8 Can			cann kan
9 Rub	rud rup		rubb wrub
10 Fox			focks foks focs phox phocks
11 Tape	pate		tayp
12 Why			wy wiye wye
13 Rise			rize ryes
14 So		sow sew	sowe
15 Note	noet		noat
16 Wish			whish
17 Moth	woth		
18 June			joon
19 Taken			takun tacon tacun takeun
20 Even			evon evan evun
21 Sigh			siy sye sie si siye syh sy
22 Chart			
23 Scorn	skron		skorn scourn skourn scorne scornn scawn schorn
24 Paw	wap	pour pore poor	por poar paur
25 String			
26 Pear	dear	pair	pare paire

* It is assumed that the following words are outside the pupils' vocabulary and therefore do not count as homophones – sac tun Wye pare mete rite

Some sample answers to aid analysis

Wrong symbol	Intrusions	Omissions	Non-phonic	Key word	
dine dene dien dim dein	ding		beclib	Din	1
fat veat valt fet vete vate	vilen veait			Vet	2
sake sack suke sace			sent	Sack	3
lup leip lesh lep lipe				Lip	4
nud mush bud	mund mond toughn			Mud	5
tol tone dune tern tan tune	tank tigt			Ton	6
happe haper	happen	hap		Happy	7
cun cane tan				Can	8
wub rab reb				Rub	9
thox foz fax	foxes foxs			Fox	10
tap tep tepe tack teap			teace	Tape	11
wou whey way			weth	Why	12
rese rose ris rine russ rice rish			were	Rise	13
saw			sare	So	14
nut not noot			newst	Note	15
with wich sish which			wert	Wish	16
mouth mof mothe mote mofe math moof	moft month		maue	Moth	17
Jon Jan Jine Joun			janeli	June	18
tacken teken tacan	tackund tanc		fane	Taken	19
ethn ever enen eathen			vean	Even	20
soy sige suy say	shy sign sight sighy		siu	Sigh	21
chut cart chet	charet		jot	Chart	22
scone scarn shorn squan sceern skoun	ston	son corn	snon	Scorn	23
pawr pow pauw parw pare puer	poren		poeu	Paw	24
strill strin		sinnt string sting	slieti	String	25
par peir pere per peer pier	pawl		penny	Pear	26

Dorcan Spelling Analysis DSA-02

Key word	Reversals	Homophones*	Correct phonic structure
27 Quite	quiet qiut		qwite cwite qwhite
28 Photo			photow fotow photoe foto fotowe
29 Eight	eihgt egith	ate	8
30 None	noen	nun	non knon knone
31 Joy			joye
32 Foot			
33 Raid	raib riad		rade raide rayed
34 Meet		meat	mete
35 Pound	pounb bound		
36 Road	roab	rowed rode	roed
37 Leak		leek	leack leeck
38 Soil	siol soli		solle soyal soyel
39 Dead	beab bead		ded
40 Thief	theif feith thife		theaf theigh
41 Cage			kage caje
42 Twice	tiwce ticwe		
43 Pension	penstoin pentoin		pention penshen pencion penshon penshion pensian
44 Right	wrihgt	write wright	rite
45 Spies		spy's	speyes spise spys spyes
46 Windy	winby		windey
47 Purple	pruple		perple perpel perpal
48 Rotted			rottid wrotted
49 Hopeful			hopefull
50 Living			liveing

Some sample answers to aid analysis

Wrong symbol	Intrusions	Omissions	Non-phonic	Key word	
quit cwit qite	witer quicly		kot	Quite	27
fattow phota phote thoto fato	foton phogto		pontago	Photo	28
eght et eghte eat eieght eaight	etie		eiget	Eight	29
nune noun naun noghn nen naun			naue	None	30
joue juy johe ji choy	joied		gou giy	Joy	31
fut fert fout forte feet				Foot	32
rad raed	rand		waine	Raid	33
met mert			med muse	Meet	34
pond pand pund	pouend	poon pown	pades mad	Pound	35
rud raed rawd read			roin	Road	36
leack lik lek lig leck lake lieck	link		leron	Leak	37
souol soel soyoll soel eail coyall sole	shoyl	soiy	froas	Soil	38
daid died dean deid	drad		deed	Dead	39
fethf fif fef feeth thef chief theith feaf fithe feef feth thieve thif	therf thefen		fane	Thief	40
kag ckaig cach cave cag cadge chage	catjer		kagr	Cage	41
twis twise twies twece twas twic twase	twins twist	twie	twoth	Twice	42
pencen penchone pensene penchen pinchan pancehn punchen penchin		pen pench pesion	pogrnd peach	Pension	43
rigt riet rit			rot	Right	44
spigs spice spis speis skies spirs	spices spist		sleusin	Spies	45
windig winde	winded winder	wide	wethr	Windy	46
purpl purpul poiple pourple perpol	purpht	purrl	pupou	Purple	47
roted roated routed rotd roited rotd	rotton		wanr	Rotted	48
hopfull hopful hopefool hopthel hapfull	grotted	hopf hofall	hotong	Hopeful	49
lifing lithing leaving		ling live		Living	50

Dorcan Spelling Analysis

NAME: DATE: CLASS: TESTER:

No.											
1											
2											
3											
4											
5											
6											
7											
8											
9											
10											
11											
12											
13											
14											
26											
27											
28											
29											
30											
31											
32											
33											
34											
35											
36											
37											
38											
39											

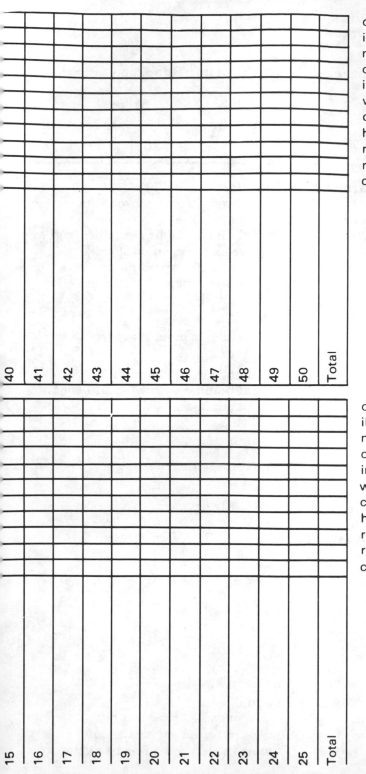

other errors
illegible
non-ph. guess
omissions
intrusions
wrong symbol
correct ph. struc.
homophone
rev. letter order
rev. letter form
correct

	40	41	42	43	44	45	46	47	48	49	50	Total

other errors
illegible
non-ph. guess
omissions
intrusions
wrong symbol
correct ph. struc.
homophone
rev. letter order
rev. letter form
correct

	15	16	17	18	19	20	21	22	23	24	25	Total

Appendix 2

Phonic source books	Workbooks	Reading stage	Level
A 1 2 3 4	1 + 2	6½–8½	1
5 6 7 8	1 + 2	8½–10½	2
9 10 11 12	1 + 2	10 +	3

Phonic source books	Phonics
Hit the Word (Introductory)	Single vowels and consonants b/d i/e a/o/u Initial blends: bl br cl cr dr fl fr gl gr pl pr sc sk sl sm sn sp st tr word ends: ck mp nd nk nt initial blend: scr word end: ll
1 A–Z of Man	initial blend: wh word ends: ft pt ed all ct th
2 Interests	initial blend: tw word ends: ng y initial blends: str scr (again) spr thr word end: lt
3 Dogs Camping	ee oo ch sh initial blend: wh (again)
4 Crooks Monsters	ea as in speak silent e
5 Circus life Stone-Age to Iron-Age Cartoons	ar or er ir ur
6 Horses Fishing Roman Britain	ai ay air oi oy o as in cold
7 Weather!	ea as in head ce ci y as in try oo as in blood
Anglo-Saxon Britain Pop music I	ge gi dge word ends: le ey as in grey ou as in found ow as in cow ow as in slow ph = f as in photo

Phonic source books Phonics

8	Fossils	ie as in f*ie*ld
		ind as in k*ind* *ild* as in w*ild*
		ould as in m*ould* *alk* as in t*alk*
	The Middle Ages	oa as in c*oa*t
		word ends: tion sion
		gu as in g*u*ess
		o as in s*o*n
	Skateboarding	*ful* as in care*ful*
9	Volcanoes	au as in h*au*l aw as in j*aw*
		io as in v*io*lent ia as in d*ia*gram
		are as in st*are* are/air-spelling
		ore as in c*ore*
	Traditions	ou as in s*ou*p uy as in b*uy* oar
		oor as in d*oor* our as in p*our*
		or/ore/aw/oar/oor/ow-spelling
		our as in fl*our*
	Tudor Britain	eer as in d*eer* ear as in d*ear*
		ear as in *ear*th ear as in b*ear*
		ear as in h*ear*t
10	UFOs	ea as in gr*ea*t ew as in n*ew*
		word ends: gh and ght
	Fashion	*sure* as in mea*sure* *ture* as in na*ture*
	Stuart Britain	wa as in *wa*nt war as in *war*d
		wor as in *wor*k wo as in *wo*men
11	Dinosaurs	silent b as in lim*b*
		silent c as in mus*c*le
	The Industrial Revolution	ch as in a*ch*e
		ch as in ma*ch*ine
	Mopeds and Motorcycles	ei as in w*ei*ght (vocabulary extension)
		silent g as in *g*nat silent k as in *k*nit
		silent w as in *w*rite silent t as in cas*t*le
12	Pop music II	y as in m*y*stery
		y as in c*y*cle (vocabulary extension)
		er as in s*er*ious ur as in c*ur*ious
	Britain from 1820	ui as in fr*ui*t
		silent p as in *p*neumonia
		word ends: ious tious tial tient cial
		cian cious xious
	The Ascent of Everest	silent n as in hym*n*
		ps as in *ps*ychology rh as in *rh*yme
		word end: gue as in fati*gue*

Reading level guide

Presentation
Print size pleasant, and
familiar fount (e.g. Schoolbook
Century, Times or Univers).

Grading:

1	2	3	4	5

Easy ⟶ Difficult

Clear headings, sub-headings
and spacing; pages turned at
sensible points. Text not too
solid.

Clear ⟶ Confusing

Illustrations that support and
explain

Explanatory → Contribute little

Vocabulary and style
Idiomatic English that flows
easily.

Idiomatic → Stilted or old-fashioned

Culturally congruous, not alien
(e.g. Public School, American).
Also age range of text and
illustrations correct, not
mismatch with pupils.

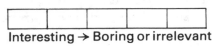
Congruous ⟶ Alien

Pupils' likely approach:
interest appeal of subject
matter before beginning
reading.

Interesting → Boring or irrelevant

Difficulty
Proportion of words of more
than 2 syllables, calculated on
100 successive words.   Under

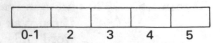

2%	3-5%	6-8%	9-11%	12%+

Proportion of abstract nouns
to concrete nouns calculated
on 10 successive nouns.

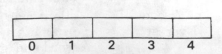

0-1	2	3	4	5

Number of clauses and
phrases in apposition in ten
sentences.

0	1	2	3	4

Answers

Codes
DEAD ON THE STROKE OF TWELVE

Ridokan Kill him tonight.

Runic Superintendent. I found this note hidden under a plate in Joe's cafe just now. I can't understand it. – Constable Holmes.

Greek Constable. I don't know this code. See if you can find any more clues. Are you sure it's serious? – Super.

Ridokan He'll be by the pine trees.

Runic Super. I have just found this note in the telephone box outside Joe's cafe. – Constable.

Greek Constable. The detective branch think you're on to a murder plot. Some of them will be joining you. Keep on searching. Look for some pine trees. – Super.

Ridokan Hide the body under the leaves.

Runic Super. Another note. This one is from the shelter for the 46 bus. – Constable.

Greek Constable. Well done. Can you see any suspicious people around? – Super.

Runic Super. No. Everyone is acting normally. – Constable.

Greek Constable. The detectives say the 46 bus does not go near any pine trees. Can you find any more clues? – Super.

Ridokan Dead on the stroke of twelve.

Runic Super. Here's another note. This one from the next bus shelter up the road. But where are the detectives? – Constable.

Greek Constable. The detectives are following their own trail. Keep looking. – Super.

Ridokan Death is all he deserves.

Runic Super. This note was on the board that says Forest Road. There are twelve pine trees at the end of the road. – Constable.

Greek Constable. Search the trees for clues. – Super.

Ridokan Beware of the Ghost. He sucks your blood with vampire teeth. Beware at twelve.

Runic Super. Here's another note. What do all these notes mean? How long until the detectives arrive? – Constable.

Greek   Constable. The last note said 'Beware of the Ghost'. The detectives will join you at twelve. – Super.

English Just after twelve the Superintendent arrives on the scene. As he comes up he hears a man's terrified scream, and then silence. He finds this unfinished note:

Runic   Super. It's ten to twelve and I've not seen anyone around. No more notes. The only new clue has been that on the twelfth str . . .

English What do you think the notes were about? What happened to the police constable? What report will the Superintendent be making?

Holiday books

p 21 – Riddles: Christmas cake
                       Christmas stocking
                       Christmas tree
                       Christmas pudding
                       carol singing

p 22 –   box of crackers

p 23 –   letter
                       television
                       bicycle
                       book

      Code: Brian brought a brittle bit of broken bottle back.
                       David's dreadful dog dragged a dead dragon down the dry ditch.
                       Philip fell flat on his freckled face in the flooded field on Friday.

p 25 – Riddles: Easter egg
                       car
                       horse

      Limericks: Dover, fast, past, over
                       dress, rip, mess

p 27 – Riddles: chair
                       comb
                       football

p 29 – Riddles: swim wear
                       sunshine
                       camera
                       waves

Anagrams:	motorway
	seaside
	campsite
	icecream
	lemonade
	cream cakes
p 31 – Limericks:	boat, why, shy, float
	door, complained, trained, floor
	stilts, down, frown, kilts
Code:	Seven shining silver shells shone in six
	shallow slots.
	Penny brought the best pretty pink
	pyjamas as a proper birthday present
	for her baby brother's birthday.

Index

Index